THE
ARAB WORLD
HANDBOOK

Arabian Peninsula and Iraq Edition
Fully Revised

THE
ARAB WORLD HANDBOOK

Arabian Peninsula and Iraq Edition
Fully Revised

STACEY INTERNATIONAL

THE
ARAB WORLD HANDBOOK
Arabian Peninsula and Iraq Edition
Fully Revised

Published by Stacey International
128 Kensington Church Street
London W8 4BH
Tel: +44 (0)20 7221 7166
Fax: +44 (0)20 7792 9288
E-mail: info@stacey-international.co.uk
Website: stacey-international.co.uk

ISBN: 978 1 906768 034

First published 2000
Second edition published 2005
Third edition published 2009

Editor: Max Scott

British Library Cataloguing-in-Publication Data
A catalogue record for this book is available
from the British Library

1 3 5 7 9 8 6 4 2

Acknowledgements

I am especially indebted to Sir John Wilton, KCMG, KCVO, MC, the Hon Ivor Lucas, CMG, Patrick de Courcy-Ireland, CVO, Miles Reinhold, the late Patrick Bannerman, Christopher Wilton, CMG, the late Hugh Tunnell, Lawrie Walker LVO, OBE and David Lloyd, OBE for their kind advice and assistance with the manuscript of this book. However, responsibility for the content and any errors is mine alone. I am indebted also to AJMC, PRMH and YIY.

Finally, I would like to express my sincere thanks to Max Scott, Kitty Carruthers and Tom Stacey of Stacey International for their invaluable contribution.

JP

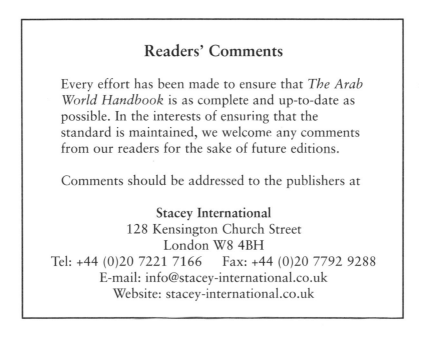

Readers' Comments

Every effort has been made to ensure that *The Arab World Handbook* is as complete and up-to-date as possible. In the interests of ensuring that the standard is maintained, we welcome any comments from our readers for the sake of future editions.

Comments should be addressed to the publishers at

Stacey International
128 Kensington Church Street
London W8 4BH
Tel: +44 (0)20 7221 7166   Fax: +44 (0)20 7792 9288
E-mail: info@stacey-international.co.uk
Website: stacey-international.co.uk

Contents

Chapter Four: Visiting the Peninsula

Chapter Five: The Expatriate

Chapter Six: The Business Traveller

Annexes

Maps

Introduction

Foreign visitors entering the region of Arabia and the Gulf for the first time will find themselves in a world that in many respects is profoundly unfamiliar. The mindset is different, at first inexplicably so. The most sympathetic person will find the scene confusing. The language is complicated, the social etiquette by which the Arabs set so much store takes time to pick up and the Muslim religion is in evidence everywhere as the major influence on daily life. Even the conduct of business has its own special rules. Finally, the whole often seems clouded by that indefinable element, the mystique of the Orient.

Few books succeed in presenting the subject in an easily understandable form, but **The Arab World Handbook**, building on the success of *Very Simple Arabia, Very Simple Arabic* and *Very Simple Arabic Script,* aims to do just that. Cutting through the mystique, it sets out the essential information needed by the short term visitor, the expatriate and business traveller. It outlines the basic elements of the culture, language and religion. The chapter on etiquette tells the foreigner how to behave in the most commonly experienced situations, and subsequent chapters give advice on the planning and conduct of a visit to the region and on living there.

The final chapter outlines the basis for commercial success, helping the business traveller to operate effectively from the outset. Competition in the region is now so keen that business travellers cannot afford to jeopardise their chances through ignorance of the basic rules. This book sets out the essential steps to achieving success.

Do not be too concerned by the amount of information you have to absorb. Read up on your immediate needs then refer back as the situation develops. Experience shows that information is much easier to assimilate once you are involved in a real-life situation.

James Peters

CHAPTER ONE

Background

GEOGRAPHY AND CLIMATE

1

The Arabian Peninsula, or Arabia as it was traditionally known, is that major part of the Arab world resembling the head of an axe, with its butt bordering on Jordan and Iraq and its cutting edge lying on the Arabian Sea and the Gulf of Aden. In the west, the Red Sea separates it from Africa and in the east, the Gulf divides it from Iran.

Geography

The Peninsula divides into two main types of terrain. One consists of rugged hills and mountains of volcanic and igneous origin. The western part of the Peninsula, inland from the Red Sea, and incorporating the Hejaz, the Asir and most of Yemen, is of this type. The Hajar mountains of Oman, including the Jebel Akhdar, is a geologically distinct but superficially similar area of rough mountains covering most of northern Oman.

The rest of the Peninsula consists of very flat and featureless expanses of sand, gravel and sedimentary rock, relieved in some places by low escarpments and dry wadi beds. The main sand deserts are the famous Empty Quarter, or *Rub'al-Khali*, in the southeast and the Great Nefud in the north.

Overall, the Peninsula tilts gradually from the heights of Yemen in the southwest, which rise in places to over 3,000 metres, down to sea level in the east and northeast. A few small areas of southwest Arabia receive enough rainfall to support extensive areas of low forest; the rest of the land surface is arid or semi-arid desert, which nonetheless is sufficiently vegetated to support extensive seasonal grazing and to sustain an interesting population of bird and animal life. Much of the scenery possesses a bleak but dramatic beauty.

The Peninsula has a reputation as a hot and dusty place, and indeed the temperature in the dry summer months of May to September can be very high, reaching 40°C on the coasts and up to 50°C in inland areas. The effects of the high temperatures are made worse by the high humidity around the coasts of the Gulf and the Red Sea in summer and early autumn. In spring and autumn the weather is pleasant with comfortable

Climate

1

temperatures, clear skies and cool breezes. Most of the scanty annual rains fall in winter when it can also be cold, especially in the heart of the Peninsula. A visitor to the region need take very little precaution against the weather, other than a sweater and an umbrella during the winter months.

More detailed information on geography and climate is given in the country annexes of this book.

HISTORICAL SUMMARY

Recent archaeological work in all parts of Arabia has demonstrated the antiquity of human settlement there. Shuwaiyhitiyah in northern Nejd is one of the world's most ancient settlement sites; thousands of other Stone Age sites across the Peninsula testify to the expansion and cultural development of the earliest Arabian.

Later, beginning about 5000 BC, we find evidence (on the Gulf coasts) of a succession of cultures – Ubaid, Dilmun, Umm al-Nar and others – which emerged under the twin stimuli of seafaring contacts between Mesopotamia and the Indus Valley, and the discovery and production of valuable resources of copper in Oman and pearls in Bahrain. On the Red Sea, copper, gold and incense were the commodities which encouraged the development of trading links and settlement along the coast.

From the earliest historical times until the 20th century, Arabia has been isolated. The harshness of the terrain has been a complete deterrent to invaders and colonisers, which has guaranteed a remarkable continuity of the ancient ways in most parts of the Peninsula. Contacts with the outside world were limited to coastal trade. Very occasional foreign military expeditions such as that of the Roman legion under Aelius Gallus, or the Ethiopian king Abraha in the 6th century AD, were rare events which left no lasting effect.

Even after the emergence of Islam, the fact that the centres of political power of the Umayyad and Abbasid empires were in Syria and Iraq meant that Arabia remained a backwater, except for the pilgrimage route to Makkah and Madinah.

Makkah, the principal destination of the pilgrim, is the city where the Prophet Muhammad was born in AD 571 and where he lived until AD 622, when he fled to Madinah. The gradual revelation to him of the Holy Quran was met by the initial scepticism and opposition of many of his fellow citizens, but by the time of his death in AD 632, the newly revealed faith of Islam was spread widely throughout Arabia. His successors, the four orthodox caliphs, continued the expansion of the faith through what is now known as the Arab world and Iran. Thereafter, the caliphate moved to Damascus and Baghdad and by AD 900 the Arab conquest and the Islamic faith extended from Spain to the borders of China. Arabia's role became politically and militarily less significant, but the pilgrimage has continued uninterrupted every year for 1,300 years, to act as an enormously important factor in welding Islamic society together. The opportunity to exchange information, to travel, to meet and talk with fellow-Muslims from distant parts of the Islamic world has always acted as a leaven in broadening the Muslim's mind and a brake on the centrifugal forces which act on any such widespread society.

> The birth of the Prophet Muhammad

The isolation of Arabia from foreign influence and interference was challenged in the 16th century by the Portuguese and the Ottoman Turks. The Portuguese wanted to consolidate their grip on the sea routes to Asia and as part of this strategy built a series of forts, most of which still exist, to control various ports around the coast, at Muscat, Bahrain and Tarut,* where they remained until late in the 17th century. Their interest was maritime, and so they affected the land and the people very little.

The Ottoman Turks had a more profound influence. After their capture of Constantinople in 1453, they rapidly took the Levant and North Africa under their control, and by 1568 had conquered Yemen and brought the holy cities of Makkah and Madinah under their control. They continued to exercise this control off and

> The Ottoman Turks

---

* see map of Saudi Arabia on page 196

1

on until the collapse of the Ottoman Empire during the First World War, and have left numerous traces of their occupation through the Hejaz, most famously the Hejaz railway. In the northern Gulf, too, they extended their influence from their province of Iraq as far as Bahrain and Al Hasa; but they never controlled the centre of Arabia. The famous military expedition of Muhammad Ali which razed the town of Dir'iyyah near Riyadh in 1818 was purely a punitive raid.

THE ANCIENT ARAB CIVILISATION

Scientifically and culturally the Arabs were at the forefront of learning during early mediaeval times, keeping alive Greek learning and eventually passing it on to Western Europe; and in the process adding much that was new in medicine, physics, astronomy and many other branches of science. As Professor Philip Hitti puts it in his *Short History of the Arabs,* 'No people in the Middle Ages contributed to human progress so much as did the Arabs...Arab scholars were studying Aristotle when Charlemagne and his lords were reportedly learning to write their names. Scientists in Cordova, with their seventeen great libraries, each alone of which included more than 400,000 volumes, enjoyed luxurious baths at a time when washing the body was considered a dangerous custom at the University of Oxford.' The Arab contribution to science is amply evidenced by the numerous Arabic words in the English language such as alchemy, alcohol, algebra, calibre, arsenal and admiral. Our star names are also largely Arabic – Rigel, Betelgeuse, Fomelhaut and many others.

Britain was the last outside power to wield influence in Arabia, primarily – like the Portuguese before them – as an adjunct to their interests further east. The colonisation of Aden, and the various treaties of protection and

1

exclusivity signed with the rulers of the Gulf states and
the Aden Protectorate, lasted until the middle years of
the 20th century, by which time all of the present states
of the Peninsula were independent and self-governing.

The discovery
of oil

Following the Second World War the politics and
economics of the region were transformed by the
exploitation of the region's vast oil resources. The
transformation wrought to the infrastructure of many
of the Arab countries since the assertion of direct control
of their oil wealth after 1973 was remarkable by any
standards. It also meant that most countries in the
Arabian Peninsula made a lightning transition into the
technological age. In recent years the trend has been
towards more measured progress, a consolidation of past
achievements and the diversification of their economies
wherever possible. Saudi Arabia, Kuwait, Qatar, Bahrain,
the United Arab Emirates and Oman form a political,
economic and military grouping known as the Gulf Co-
operation Council (GCC) and, with the exception of
Oman, are also members of the Organisation of Arab
Petroleum Exporting Countries (OAPEC), as is Iraq.
All the countries of the Peninsula and Iraq are members
of the Arab League. (*See* the Annexes for Regional
Organisations and information on individual countries
of the Peninsula.)

Various terms are used to describe the region and it is
as well to be aware of some possible local sensitivities in
this regard. The term 'Middle East' finds less favour in
the Peninsula region because it was conceived in the West
and lumps the cultures and peoples of the Arab world
together as one, whereas the Gulf Arabs feel that their
culture is distinctively different. It is better to refer to
the Arab world, the Arabian Peninsula and Gulf Arabs.
Secondly, although the Gulf itself has commonly been
described as the Persian Gulf, and some may refer to it
as the Arabian Gulf, it is simpler to refer to it as the Gulf.
Finally, when Arabs talk of the Gulf States they generally
mean Bahrain, Kuwait, Qatar, the UAE, Saudi Arabia
and Oman – i.e. the GCC states. If in doubt, it is best to
specify which countries you are referring to by name.

Terminololgy

1

CULTURE AND SOCIETY

Despite the introduction of Western technology and consumer products, all of which have had a marked modernising influence on Arab life, the culture of the Peninsula countries retains its own distinctively Arab character.

The Desert Tradition

The Bedu

Although it is fast disappearing, the way of life of the nomadic Bedu (*sing*. Bedouin), the inhabitants of the desert hinterland, is the basis of today's Arabian culture. It has remained unchanged for centuries. The Bedu are superbly adapted to the harsh desert conditions in which they tend their flocks of sheep and goats, supported by their other lifeline, the camel. The camel provides them with milk, meat, material for their clothing, tents, and transport. The staple diet of the Bedu is dates, flour, camel's or goat's milk and meat from their flocks. Their clothing, ideally suited to the heat, is a long loose shirt and headcloth. They are hardy, self-reliant and fiercely independent. In the past, armed with rifle and sword and mounted on horseback, they raided other Bedu tribes and camel caravans, capturing their livestock and possessions. Although interdependent with the settled folk in the towns and village, the Bedu have always considered themselves superior.

The Bedu way of life

At the core of Bedu society lies the concept of the tribe, which has its own strict hierarchy. Some of the tribes were renowned for a particular expertise – such as camel-breeding, fighting or tracking. The tribes dominated a territorial area, usually designated by water wells which were jealously guarded against all comers. Each tribe was then subdivided into clans, consisting of a number of families and led by a Shaikh who was elected by consensus. Although the position of Shaikh was not always passed from father to son as of right, it tended to stay within the same family.

The daily life of the Bedu is governed by a time-honoured and strict code of conduct, with set procedures for the settlement of inter-tribal disputes and the punishment of crimes. Traditionally, each member of the tribe had a direct right of access to the Shaikh, with whom he could converse on equal terms. Deference is always shown to the elders in the community, and the poor are cared for. On an individual level, a Bedouin's word is his bond, the rule of hospitality inviolable, and his loyalty to family and tribe is of paramount importance. These values were equally shared by the settled foundations of Arabia.

This emphasis on family loyalty and the importance of the extended family continues today – grandparents, parents and children often living together in one house. Men and women have separate quarters. A male foreigner who is privileged to be invited to an Arab home would not normally meet the womenfolk but he might be surprised to learn of the enormous influence they exert behind the scenes. Although Islam permits four wives, most Arabs these days have only one. If a man has more than one wife, the Holy Quran rules that they must all be treated equally.

Values

Although the Arabs of the region are increasingly aware of Western culture through the media and through frequent travel to the West – and indeed many are educated in the West, own property and have business interests there as well – there is a strong desire to protect the Arab and Islamic culture. They accept the inevitability of change, but wish it to take place slowly and in a controlled manner, enabling them among other things to avoid the unacceptable elements.

The traditional Arab values of honourable behaviour, courtesy and unfailing hospitality survive. Honouring his word, loyalty to the family, respect for age, and the care of the poor continue to be a major influence on an Arab's way of life. He is by tradition a very proud and dignified person; status, influence and appearances matter. Although modest himself, he does not admire those who fail to exercise their authority or are self-deprecating. The Arab is none the less sensitive – personal remarks about

The Arab
character

1

Friendship

his honour, family or Faith, however light-hearted, could well cause offence. Conscious of recent history and the considerable influence wielded by the Western powers in the region, the Arab is not unnaturally sensitive to anything which could be interpreted as exploiting his position or is in any way patronising. He expects to be dealt with fairly and on equal terms.

The people of the Gulf tend to be demonstrative, tactile and unafraid of emotion. The elaborate courtesies of Arab etiquette may seem exaggerated, but the reserve of Westerners often strikes the Arab as coldness. They do not have our shyness of physical contact and men often hold hands in public as a simple mark of friendship. They shake hands a great deal and may hold on to someone's hand long after shaking it. This is a demonstration of friendship and it would be unfriendly to withdraw it. It is commonplace for Arabs to embrace relatives, close friends, dignitaries and members of a ruling family when they meet them and kiss them symbolically on the cheeks, forehead or nose (depending on the relationship and local custom), but an Arab would have to know a Westerner extremely well before greeting him in this way.

The traditional recreations are as keenly pursued today as they ever were. The Shaikhly sport of falconry is still highly popular.

Camels are still widely owned and are bred for racing, which is a major public sporting event.

Personal Relationships

Arabs are distinguished by being friendly, courteous and hospitable. They set great store by personal relationships. The custom of greeting, shaking hands and asking after someone's health is more than mere formality. The enquiries are often searching and evidence a genuine desire to know of one's well-being and that of one's family.

The establishment of good personal relationships is crucial to success in any dealings in the Peninsula, something which many foreign organisations are even now slow to recognise. Whereas in the West a friendship

1

THE ARAB HORSE

The Arab passion for horses is well known. The Bedu were first attracted to the horse by its speed and agility which made it particularly suitable for raiding and warfare. The famous Arab horse originated in the Nejd region of Saudi Arabia and by the 6th century AD they had succeeded in breeding strains which were subsequently used to improve stock throughout Europe and elsewhere. The Arab horse of today is still characterised by its beauty, agility, speed and stamina. Michael Clayton, editor of *Horse and Hound*, writes: 'The origins of the [British] Thoroughbred were in Arabia... Three stallions are credited with the creation of the Thoroughbred in the late seventeenth and early eighteenth centuries: the Godolphin Arabian, the Darley Arabian and the Byerley Turk. None ran a race, but they sired stock and all modern Thoroughbreds descend from them in the male line.'

may develop from a successful business deal, in the Arab world the reverse is true. The degree of success in establishing a rapport depends on one's character, but someone who is polite and sensitive, staightforward and open, is likely to succeed. Perhaps the single most important additional quality that an Arab will look for is integrity.

A meaningful relationship in the Peninsula takes time to establish. It may take months or even years. The process may be shortened slightly if the newcomer is personally recommended to an Arab or if their standing and reputation are well known, but an Arab will still wish to make his own independent judgement.

If you think you get on well with Arabs be careful not to overdo it. Some foreigners become over familiar or attempt to imitate the Arab way of life. Experience shows that this can lead to contempt or may even offend. The

Establishing
a rapport

1

outsider who gets on best is the person who, while respecting the Arab way of life, maintains a respectful distance from it.

Arab Women

The special situation with regard to women in the region is one of the most difficult for a foreigner to understand. The apparent domination of men and the seclusion of women is sometimes criticised by Westerners, who judge what they see by their own standards. They would do well to remind themselves that they are dealing with a radically different culture and moral code.

Women in the Arab world are not judged inferior to men. That may have been the case before Islam but an important aspect of the Faith is that the rights of women are protected. In the Peninsula, Arab women, who have always been influential in private life, now play an increasingly important role in public life as well. The seclusion of women is, however, a long-standing tradition in Arabia and one that remains strong. The degree of seclusion varies from country to country. In most, it is still strictly followed. Arab women live in separate quarters and are not seen by male visitors. Throughout the Peninsula, when appearing in public, it is commonplace to see women wearing the traditional long black cloak (*abaya*) and head shawl either with all of the face except the eyes covered (*hijab*) or with a mask covering the lower part of the face (*burqa'*). Women pray separately from men. You will also see wives walking behind their husbands. Women may go shopping alone, but if they visit a friend or appear in public they will often be accompanied by their husband or chaperoned by a brother. In Saudi Arabia women are required to cover their arms and legs in public (*see General Comments* in the Saudi Arabia Annex) and are not at present permitted to drive cars. In other countries of the Peninsula you may find many women apparently behaving very much as they do in the West, wearing Western clothes (perhaps with a head shawl) and driving cars. Nevertheless, the fundamental custom of

Seclusion
of women

seclusion still applies and in all other respects they would behave as described above.

Although you may hear that in Islam a man may divorce his wife simply by renouncing her, it is seldom practised and divorce is by no means as common as in the West. A divorced man must make full financial and other provision for his ex-wife. In addition, an Arab woman may own property, inherit goods and money and a wife's individual possessions are always protected – she does not have to share them with her husband.

Divorce

It is less well known that even in the most conservative of households women are often the power behind the throne, that although marriages arc often arranged, the bride is still free to decline to marry someone if she wishes. Whatever happens, a woman can usually find out a lot about her prospective husband before a decision on marriage is taken and modern reforms have secured the eradication of any discriminatory practices in the marriage agreement.

Modern Arab women have travelled further afield and are better informed through newspapers, radio, television and films than were their forbears. The most significant advance in recent years, as with men, has been in education. Women are now able to play an increasingly wide role in society in a variety of occupations. These are currently in the teaching profession (girls' schools and universities), in medicine (as nurses and doctors), television and radio, light industry and, in rural communities, agriculture. There are also a number of highly successful Arab businesswomen, and lawyers, and others who have risen to the highest echelons of government.

The modern Arab woman

Male visitors to the Peninsula should, of course, always show great respect for the seclusion of women. And the same applies if they meet an Arab woman abroad. An Arab woman may be dressed in a Western style but one must not assume she may be treated as a Westerner. To take any liberty could have serious repercussions.

23

1

Headdress

Dress

For the Arabs of the Peninsula the traditional male dress is a long loose garment called variously a *thobe* or *dishdasha*. Of fine white cotton in summer, it is ideally suited to the hot climate. In winter, it is of heavier weave and may be augmented by a brown or black cloak (a *bisht* or *mishla*) or sometimes with a jacket or overcoat. The *bisht* of a senior citizen or member of a ruling family might be trimmed with gold braid. In the Arab Gulf countries and Saudi Arabia a head cloth (a *ghūtra* or *shemaag*) is also worn and kept in place with a black rope (an *aqaal*). A white cotton head cloth is usual in summer and a thicker cloth in winter, patterned either in red-and-white or green-and-white. In one variation of style, fashionable with the younger generation, the head cloth is worn wrapped around the head without the rope and in another variant strict followers of Islam wear the red-and-white patterned head cloth loose over the head, again without the head rope. Such religious men may also cultivate a large untrimmed beard and shortened *thobe*. In Yemen and sometimes Oman the head cloth is wrapped tightly round the head or piled high like a turban. The most common headgear in Oman however, is a small round woven hat (*qūbba'a*) worn in a variety of colours and decorations.

LANGUAGE, LITERATURE AND ART

Because the Holy Quran was revealed by the Archangel Gabriel to the Prophet Muhammad in Arabic, the language is esteemed by Muslims as the language of God. Arabic is the official language of the Peninsula although English is also widely used and understood.

Arab literature is dominated by the writings of the Holy Quran, by poetry and prose. The Holy Quran is neither prose nor poetry but is universally considered by Muslims to be a work of unsurpassable excellence. The true meaning and sound can only be appreciated in the original. Although at one time translation was

1

forbidden as an irreverent act, the Holy Quran has now been translated into several languages, including English, for the benefit of the many non-Arab Muslims in the world.

In art, the Holy Quran has been interpreted as forbidding the portrayal of the human form, at least in decorating religious buildings. As a result, the art style in the Arab world developed from decorative floral and geometric forms and evolved into the unique interwoven recurrent motifs of abstract design known as Arabesque. This explains the almost total absence of naturalistic or representational art which is so much a part of art in other cultures. Another extremely popular form of Arab art is calligraphy and various forms of the Arabic script are used to decorate pottery, glass and metalwork with dense but highly organised and skilfully executed designs.

In the Peninsula the architectural style is distinct from the rest of the Arab world. Traditional buildings use local materials – clay, stone, gypsum are plain and undecorated, and rely on form and volume for their beauty. The Red Sea towns used more coral stone and timber in their construction and are generally more elegant than central and eastern Arabian towns. Weaving, pottery and other crafts also have a simple functional beauty far removed from their sophisticated urban equivalents in Cairo, Istanbul or Damascus.

Arab craftsmanship

GOVERNMENT AND BUSINESS

The States of the Arabian Peninsula, in their present form, came into existence in the last 78 years. In nearly all countries one finds that one or other tribe or family occupies the dominant political position and all, barring Yemen and Iraq, are monarchies. The political power-base generally lies in the hands of the senior members of the ruling family, other leading families (particularly the leading merchant families) and the armed forces. The rulers (or in the case of Yemen, the President) are assisted in government by a consultative council and/or

Political power

1

Cabinet. Bahrain and Kuwait also have elected National Assemblies. The routine of government is carried out by the tried and tested traditional system of consultation by the ruler and executed by the Cabinet and Government Ministers. Members of the ruling family usually hold the key ministerial appointments such as defence, foreign affairs and the interior.

Bureaucracy

Although the newcomer to the region will probably find the apparent bureaucracy of government similar to his own, the procedures will be new to him and may seem excessively ponderous. Expatriates and business travellers find it eminently sensible to enlist the aid of a local representative to help them deal with routine, but time-consuming, procedures. If you attempt to do things on your own and encounter difficulties, do not lose your cool, do not attempt to brow-beat anyone and do not even consider attempting to bribe a government official. It is considered a serious offence.

The decision-makers

The non-routine decision-making process in a Peninsula government or institution is usually tightly controlled by a surprisingly small number of high-ranking people. The decision-maker may have a large number of seemingly influential subordinates but even relatively minor decisions have to be referred to the top. This may be frustrating, but only patience and local advice will help you determine if you can short-cut the system. It is always in a Westerner's interest to get along with the subordinates in an organisation and such a tightly controlled system also has the advantage that major decisions can sometimes be made remarkably quickly, cutting through all obstacles and allowing swift implementation of a project. In recent years the bureaucratic system of boards and committees who investigate, consider and report has been increasingly introduced as an aid to decision-taking in the public sector, although the final decision still has to be made at the top level.

Finally, the pace of life in the Arab world is slower than in the West. This is not inefficiency but simply the result of a difference in outlook. It is not sensible to attempt to keep to a tight schedule on a visit to the region. (*See* Chapter 3 – *The Arab Perception of Time*).

LAW, ORDER AND DECORUM

Theoretical Islam and the Islamic law (*Shari'a*), based on the Holy Quran and the *Hadith* (authenticated teachings, sayings and actions of the Prophet Muhammad), provide the basis for every aspect of modern life. In practice, the administrative needs of the modern state result in an increasing amount of legislation and regulation in the fields of finance, commerce, defence, health, education, social security, etc. In religious, family and social affairs, however, the influence of Islam remains predominant and is the more jealously defended as society witnesses the increase in what are seen as Western influences and the demands of the contemporary state. The defence of traditional Islamic values against the social and economic values of the West is a prime factor in the reassertion of Islam. In particular, the orderly and law-abiding characteristics of Muslim society are contrasted with the violence and degeneration seen in contemporary Western society. Standards of dress, laws against blasphemy and the prohibition on alcohol and drugs are being strictly enforced and foreign visitors should take care in this regard. (*See* Chapter 4 – *Standards of Dress; Prohibited Goods*, and Chapter 5 – *Local Laws and Customs*.)

Arabs are generally law-abiding and the Arab countries traditionally safe places in which to live. However, in the current political climate, Westerners are obliged to pay serious attention to the question of personal security and particularly to the advice issued by their governments. This subject is covered in more detail in Chapters 4, 5 and 6 and in the Country Annexes, which also contain important details of the local law in individual countries.

ISLAM

Islam is all-pervasive in Arabia. A visitor who knows nothing of it will find it difficult to understand the

Shari'a law

1

society he has come across, since its teachings govern so much of the daily life of the people of Arabia.

Islam

Translated from the Arabic, the word Islam means 'submission to the will of God'. Thus a Muslim is one who submits. Islam consists of three essential elements. The first and most important is faith and belief in God and in the fact that Muhammad was His Prophet, the last in the line of prophets, through whom the definitive revelation was made. These central beliefs are repeated five times a day in the call to prayer. The second element is a respect for the rites of worship and the revealed law (known as *Shari'a*). The Holy Quran, the record of God's revelation through the Prophet Muhammad, is the primary source of these obligations, but is supplemented as a source of law by the *Hadith*, which are collections of reports of the deeds and sayings of the Prophet Muhammad. Thirdly, Islam imposes an obligation of virtue and excellence in the way the Muslim leads his life.

THE HOLY QURAN

The physical entity of the Holy Quran as a book carries a sanctity and reverence as the direct revelation of God to the Prophet Muhammad. In a Muslim home it often rests on a special stand. A non-Muslim visitor should not handle it without permission. God's revelation to the Prophet Muhammad is set out in 114 *Suras*, or chapters. Included within its pages are detailed prescriptions of personal and social conduct covering such things as moral standards, divorce, food, drink and the treatment of prisoners.

The Arabic word for God is *Allah* and the Muslim's creed is expressed in the brief statement:

La illaha illa Allah. Mūhammad Rasool Allah!
(There is) no god but the God (and) Muhammad (is the) Messenger of God!

The Holy Quran occupies a very different place in Islam from that of the Bible in Christianity. For one thing, it reproduces the very word of God as spoken in Arabic through the Prophet Muhammad. It is agreed by Arabs to be the most powerful and most beautiful work in the Arabic language, affecting readers and listeners with the power of its language in a way which non-Arabic speakers find impossible to share. The language is in places plain and straightforward in meaning, in others elliptical and poetic.

Any copy of the Holy Quran is treated with great respect; non-Muslims should not handle one without permission, and will give offence if they show any disrespect to it.

The speech of an Arab Muslim is full of references to God. There are dozens – even hundreds – of expressions in everyday speech which invoke the name of Allah. Perhaps the best known is the expression '*In-sha'Allah*' – if God wills – which is usually added to the expression of any future intention. This is not just a formulaic religious sentiment; the speaker believes that it is a necessary qualification of his intention. When you say to an Arab that you will see him at 9 a.m. the next day, and he replies '*In-sha'Allah*', show him that you respect this belief by not commenting on it. The correct response is '*In-sha'Allah*'.

A feature of Islam which will be evident to a visitor to the Peninsula is the extent to which so many aspects of daily life are regulated by precise directions. These directions stem from the Quran and *Hadith*, and are therefore not changeable. Whereas Christianity sets out general moral principles against which actions may be judged, and the law in a Christian society may be amended as circumstances change, Islam and the *Shari'a* are indissolubly linked, and any prescriptions in them may not be altered. So the laws of the *Shari'a* tell a Muslim precisely how and when to worship; they cover eating and drinking; marriage, divorce and inheritance; they define honourable behaviour and stipulate how a person should act towards the poor, prisoners and

The will of Allah

1

orphans; they lay down penalties for crimes; they govern tax, capital and the return on capital; and many things besides. To unfamiliar eyes, this may appear as an irksomely restrictive system, but to the Muslim their unchanging nature gives him a comfortable feeling that he knows where he stands.

The newcomer to the region will hear mention of various groupings within Islam and in particular of the Sunni and the Shi'a. This division originated in a disagreement after the death of the Prophet over the question of who should succeed him as Caliph (from the Arabic *khaleefa* or 'successor'), between those who favoured an elected Caliph and chose Abu Bakr, the Prophet's closest companion and father-in-law and those who wanted it to be the Prophet's son-in-law, Ali. The former group became known as Sunni from the Arabic word *sunna* meaning 'customary or orthodox procedure' and the latter as Shi'a, from the Arabic *shi'at ali* – the 'Party of Ali'.

The large majority of the world's 900 million Muslims are Sunni but the Shi'a are the predominant group in Iran and comprise a majority of the population in Iraq and Bahrain. There are also significant Shi'a minorities in Kuwait, UAE, Yemen and the Eastern Province of Saudi Arabia and numbers in most other Arab countries.

The doctrines of the Shi'a do not differ greatly from those of the Sunni although the Shi'a emphasise the spiritual authority of their *imams* (from the Arabic 'he who goes before'), who lead Muslims in prayer and of certain others in the Islamic hierarchy. It would be wrong to attach too much importance to this division. As one might expect in a religion of so many adherents, different schools of thought have also emerged within the Sunni and Shi'a groupings themselves – notably, as far as the Peninsula is concerned, the Muwahhidoon, a Sunni group predominant in Saudi Arabia and the Zaidis, a Shi'a group with a significant presence in Yemen. A further, independent group, the Ibadhis, are predominant in Oman.

The Five Pillars of Islam

There are five obligatory acts required of every Muslim:

- The Declaration of Faith *(Shahaada)*
- Prayer *(Salah)*
- Almsgiving *(Zakat)*
- Fasting *(Sawm)*
- The Pilgrimage to Makkah *(Hajj)*

(1) **The Declaration of Faith** (*Shahaada* – lit. 'bearing witness')
To testify to the unity of God and that Muhammad is His Prophet.

(2) **Prayer** (*Salah*)
To observe the five daily prayers at the following times: at dawn, at noon, in late afternoon, at sunset, and at night.

Worship is preceded by ablutions (*wūdooh*) when the worshipper washes his head, arms and feet with water. If no water is available, for example in the desert, then a symbolic ablution is performed with sand. The prayer, which must be said facing in the direction of Makkah, consists of between two and four sections, with a prologue and an epilogue. It is performed in several attitudes – sitting, standing, bowing and with the forehead touching the ground. The direction of Makkah is usually indicated in hotel rooms in the Peninsula and even on aircraft of Peninsula airlines.

The mosque (*masjid* – 'a place of prostration') is the place of public prayer. Although worship may be performed anywhere it is preferably done in a mosque. The worshipper may also pray wherever he happens to be at the time of prayer provided the place is clean and relatively undisturbed. A prayer rug is often used to cover the ground. The visitor to the Arab world should not be surprised when he sees prayers being performed in offices, in the airport

Prayer

31

lounge, on aircraft or on the street. This is normal practice. Do not walk in front of someone in prayer or take special notice of them.

The call to prayer is chanted by the *muezzin* from the minaret (*manaara*) which is the tall tower of the mosque. You will hear the call to prayer chanted as follows:

>1. *Allahu akbar!*
>God is most great!
>2. *Ash-hadu an la illaha illa Allah!*
>I testify that there is no god but the God!
>3. *Ash-hadu anna Mūhammad Rasool Allah!*
>I testify that Muhammad is the messenger of God!
>4. *Hayy ala-as-salah!*
>Come to prayer!
>5. *Hayy ala-al-falah!*
>Come to salvation!
>*As-salaa khairun min an-nawm!*
>Prayer is better than sleep! (said only at dawn prayer)
>6. *Allahu akbar!*
>God is most great!
>7. *La illaha,illa Allah!*
>There is no god but the God!

(Lines are repeated twice except the first, which is called four times, and the last which is called once)

On entering a mosque, Muslims remove their shoes, keep their heads covered and perform a minor ablution (*wūdooh*) before prayer. Inside the mosque there is a niche (*mihraab*) in one wall which indicates the direction of the holy city of Makkah. There is also a pulpit (*minbar*) from which the oration is given at the public prayers held at noon each Friday. The public prayer in the mosque is led by the *Imaam* (the local religious leader). Except within the principal Shia group, the Ithna-Asharis, there is no hierarchy of priests in Islam as in Christianity. The mosque is attended mainly by men. Women either pray at home or use the special place allotted to them in most large mosques.

(3) **Almsgiving** (*Zakat*)
Each year, all Muslims must pay *zakat* to help the poor. This is traditionally a fixed proportion of their savings (2.5 per cent) and is usually paid in money rather than in kind.

(4) **Fasting** (*Sawm*)
Each year throughout the holy month of Ramadan, the ninth month in the Muslim calendar, Muslims observe a fast. (By the Gregorian calendar the month of Ramadan moves forward eleven or twelve days each year.) The fast commemorates the month of the revelation of the first verses of the Holy Quran to the Prophet Muhammad and the victory of the Muslims over the Makkans at the Battle of Badr in AD 624. Between sunrise and sunset the Muslim abstains from food, drink and all pleasurable pursuits. This can be a great burden, especially in summer. Working hours are always curtailed during Ramadan. Naturally, a business traveller should take this into consideration when planning any visit to the Arab world. A non-Muslim visiting an Arab country during Ramadan should not eat, drink or smoke in the presence of a Muslim in daylight hours. After sunset the fast is broken with a substantial meal to which guests are frequently invited. Arab dignitaries break the fast with a light meal and then preside over a reception (*majlis*) at home with their families to which friends, colleagues and acquaintances pay brief visits. A Westerner who knows a particular dignitary should certainly consider visiting him on such an occasion. He should enter, shake hands with his host and other guests and sit down as indicated by his host. As new arrivals enter, follow the advice on *Seating* in Chapter 3. After refreshments, it is customary to leave, but you

Ramadan

1

may be honoured by an invitation to stay to the second, more substantial, evening meal served towards 10 p.m. In certain cases you may find the reception combined with a meal. Ramadan ends with a festival called *Eid Al-Fitr*. Muslims wear their finest clothes and gather in the mosques to pray, after which they celebrate with visits to each other's houses and hold parties. The correct behaviour for the foreigner on this occasion is explained in Chapter 3: Etiquette.

(5) **The Pilgrimage to Makkah** (*the Hajj*)

The Pilgrimage

It is obligatory for every Muslim once in his lifetime, provided that he can afford it and his health allows, to make the pilgrimage to Makkah. This takes place during the twelfth month of the Muslim year.

For the pilgrimage, the Muslim exchanges his normal dress for two plain sheets of white cloth, to demonstrate that all believers are equal before God. On arrival in Makkah he performs various ceremonies. He must first circle the Ka'aba seven times. The Ka'aba, an immense stone cube shrouded in black cloth with the sacred Black Stone in one corner, is situated in the Great Mosque in Makkah. It is the most important shrine in Islam. The pilgrim then moves outside the town and journeys seven times between two small hills, acting out the frantic search of Abraham's wife Hagar, hunting for water for her son Ishmael.

The Mount of Mercy in the Plain of Arafat is the next stop for the pilgrim, where he stands and meditates from midday to just before sunset. Finally, he goes to Mina to carry out the stoning of the three pillars, an act symbolic of the casting out of devils, and then goes on to sacrifice an animal.

The pilgrimage ends with the most important of all Muslim festivals – the *Eid Al-Adha*, or Feast of Sacrifice. This is celebrated in the same way as the *Eid Al-Fitr* except that presents and parties are more lavish. At the time of both *Eids*, greeting cards are sent to friends and acquaintances (*see* Chapter 3).

1

Traditionally, a sheep or goat is slaughtered in remembrance of the willingness of the Prophet Abraham to sacrifice his son Ishmael. Some of the food is shared with the poor and the rest is eaten at family feasts. A man who has performed the *Hajj* is called *Hajji* or *Hajj* (pilgrim) and may include the title *Hajj* in his name, generally as a prefix. Similarly a woman may call herself *Hajja*.

The Islamic Calendar, Festivals and the Working Week
The official start of the Muslim era is the year of the *Hijra* (meaning 'the migration') in AD 622 when the Prophet Muhammad, as a result of persecution while preaching God's message in Makkah, fled to Madinah. The Muslim calendar begins on the day after this flight. The Muslim year, known as *Anno Hijra* (AH), is based on twelve lunar months. These lunar months are shorter than the months of the Gregorian calendar and overall the Muslim year is shorter than the Gregorian by some eleven days. The Hejirian calendar is used today for all religious purposes and in Saudi Arabia for all official purposes as well. The Muslim date is often printed beside the Gregorian date in Arab documents.

Islamic calendar

The days of the week in Arabic are:

Saturday	*Yome as-sabt*
Sunday	*Yome al-ahad*
Monday	*Yome al-ithnain*
Tuesday	*Yome al-thalaatha*
Wednesday	*Yome al-arba'a*
Thursday	*Yome al-khamees*
Friday	*Yome al-jūm'a*

Days of the week

The twelve months of the Islamic calendar, each of 29 or 30 days are:

1. *Mūharram*
2. *Safar*
3. *Rabee al-awwal*

35

1

Islamic
months

4. *Rabee al-**thaa**nee*
5. *Jūmaada al-ūwla*
6. *Jūmaada al-**thaa**nee*
7. *Rajab*
8. *Sha'aban*
9. *Rama**dan***
10. ***Shaww**aal*
11. *Dhū al-**qi'da***
12. *Dhū al-**hijj**ah*

The various festivals and celebrations in the Muslim calendar are given on page 37. However, apart from the *Eid Al-**Adha*** and the *Eid Al-Fitr*, not all of them are celebrated in every country in the region. In Saudi Arabia, for example, only the *Eid Al-**Adha*** and the *Eid Al-Fitr* are public holidays.

It is traditional in the region to take one's annual holiday during the hottest part of the summer and at the same time as the schools' summer holiday. This period runs from about mid-July to mid-September.

In most countries the working week is from Sunday to Thursday, although Thursday is a half-day for Government institutions and schools. In Saudi Arabia and Yemen however, it runs from Saturday to Wednesday. Friday is the holy day set aside for communal worship when all Muslims attend the Mosque. For everyone living in the region Friday is a day of rest and one of the greatest *faux pas* for a Westerner is to ring someone in the Peninsula on a Friday.

The working
week

The daily routine in the region, particularly during the summer, is to work from quite early in the morning until early afternoon, break for a siesta at lunchtime, and resume work for a few hours in the late afternoon or evening. Government offices are usually only open in the first half of the day. The above hours are often extended in the winter.

During the month long fast of Ramadan working hours are severely curtailed, particularly towards the end of the month, and shop opening times become erratic, opening for a few hours in the morning and

1

MUSLIM FESTIVALS

Annual Festival	Approximate dates			
	2009	2010	2011	2012
Lailat Al-Mi'raj (The Prophet's night journey to heaven)	20 July	9 July	29 Jun	17 Jun
Holy fast of Ramadan	22 Aug	11 Aug	1 Aug	20 June
Eid Al-Fitr (The end of Ramadan)	20 Sep	10 Sept	30 Aug	19 Aug
*Eid Al-**Adh**a* (The Feast of Sacrifice)	27 Nov	16 Nov	6 Nov	26 Oct
Ras As-Sana (The Muslim New Year)	18 Dec	7 Dec	26 Nov	15 Nov
Ashura (A Shia festival)	27 Dec	16 Dec	5 Dec	24 Nov
Mawlid An-Nabi (The Prophet Muhammad's Birthday)	9 Mar	26 Feb	15 Feb	4 Feb

Because the Muslim calendar follows the lunar cycle all these dates will be some 11 days earlier in each subsequent year. The actual date of a festival depends on the sighting of the moon and that may vary from place to place by a day or two.

then for extended periods at night after the fast has been broken.

A range of Middle East diaries and organisers both the Gregorain and Hejirian calendars is published by Nicholas Smith International Limited. These include the dates of public and religious holidays. Website: www.nicholas-smith.com.

CHAPTER TWO

The Arabic Language

INTRODUCTION

Arabic is a Semitic language, the family which includes Hebrew, Aramaic (the language of Jesus), Syriac and Ethiopic. Originally confined to the northern part of Arabia its use spread during the Arab conquests to the whole of the region. There are in addition many Arabic words in Farsi (Persian), Urdu, and the languages of the Mediterranean and African countries. Familiarity with Arabic extends to the wider Muslim community in other parts of the world. The Arabic script is used with modifications in Farsi and Urdu. All are written from right to left.

As the writings of the Holy Quran were revealed by God to the Prophet Muhammad in Arabic, the language has a sacred quality for Muslims. Arabic is the official language of all the Peninsula States.

There are significant differences between written and spoken Arabic. Written or so-called literary Arabic closely resembles the classical language which is enshrined in the Holy Quran. This is the Arabic used in newspapers, books, radio broadcasts and speeches. Classical Arabic has an extensive and highly descriptive vocabulary and an attractive turn of phrase.

The spoken language on the other hand differs considerably from country to country, each one having its own variation or dialect. Within the Peninsula however, the variations are not as marked as between the Peninsula and North Africa. What tends to happen when two Arabs with differing dialects meet is that they revert to the literary or classical language.

It is generally accepted that it is only possible to understand another culture if you speak the language. (Imagine how difficult it would be for a visitor to understand the British or American culture without some command of English). But few visitors to the region have the time or the opportunity for the concentrated course necessary to attain a reasonable degree of fluency. And what, some might ask, is the point of learning Arabic if English is as widely spoken as it is by the Arabs of the Peninsula?

Classical Arabic

Spoken Arabic

41

2

Yet there are good reasons for mastering a little Arabic. For anyone who is serious about getting on with Arabs it gives an excellent impression. The Arabs know how difficult it is to learn and are therefore delighted when a foreigner makes the effort. It is worth learning the essential courtesies to use when meeting and greeting people and a relatively small effort can earn a disproportionate amount of kudos and appreciation. A smattering of Arabic is also useful in a taxi or the bazaar.

THE LANGUAGE OF THE ANGELS

Arabic, spoken throughout the Arab world by some 120 million people and the religious language of an estimated 700 to 800 million Muslims in 60 different countries, is enshrined in the Holy Quran, the message revealed by the Archangel Gabriel to the Prophet Muhammad. For this reason Arabic is revered by Muslims as sacred, the language of God. The classical or literary Arabic derived from the Holy Quran is rich in vocabulary, breadth of description, hyperbole, metaphor, rhythm and rhyme. When the classical language is recited from the Holy Quran, in poetry or in prose, together with its case endings (accusative, nominative and genitive), the way in which the literary eloquence and power of expression excites the senses of the Arabs has to be experienced to be believed.

The basic pleasantries and some useful phrases are given later in this chapter and in my *Very Simple Arabic*. There are also a variety of good courses run by such institutions as the School of African and Oriental Studies (SOAS) Language Centre at the University of London, (website: www.soas.ac.uk/languagecentre) or seek advice from the Institute of Translation and Interpreting (website: www.iti.org.uk).

Language courses

Any language course must be carefully structured and sympathetically taught if the student is not to be

2

confused or demoralised. In the case of Arabic it is also better to learn a spoken form with a strong classical bias such as is used in this book.

PRONUNCIATION

Because few people have time to learn the Arabic script, most Arabic phrase books use English transliteration, and this book is no exception. All but a few Arabic letters or sounds have an equivalent in English but those which do not are shown below:

Transliteration	**pronounced as**
aa	a in father
ow	ow in how
ū	u in put
dh	th in the
ch	ch in Scottish loch
gh	r in French rue
ei	eye
q	a guttural k
'(apostrophe)	a glottal stop

There is no *p* or *v* in Arabic and an Arab will substitute *b* and *f* respectively (i.e. Peters is pronounced *Beeters* and Victor is pronounced *Fictor*).

Doubled consonants should be given double emphasis. Stressed syllables are shown in bold type. The definite article *Al* is linked to its noun or adjective by a hyphen. There is no indefinite article in Arabic.

No transliteration of Arabic can ever capture the true sounds. My aim is to give as close an approximation as possible, but as in learning any language, the reader should imitate the sounds he hears actually spoken.

Most beginners are naturally shy of pronouncing words which are totally strange to them. But speak out confidently. It does not matter if you sound a bit odd; Arabs are used to hearing a wide variety of accents from within the Arab world. They will be delighted that you have made the effort. Don't take correction

2

as criticism – it will improve your fluency and will help to establish a rapport. So the general rule for a beginner is 'Have a go!'

GREETINGS AND PLEASANTRIES

Good morning

Greeting *Sabaah al-khair* (lit. Morning the good)
Reply *Sabaah an-noor* (lit. Morning the light)

Good afternoon/
evening

Greeting *Masaa al-khair*
Reply *Masaa an-noor*

General greeting
(at any time)

Greeting *As-salaam alaykūm* (Peace be with you)
Reply *Wa alaykūm as-salaam* (And with you be peace)

Hello

Greeting *Muruhuba*
Reply *Muruhuba,* or *muruhubatayn* (two hellos) or
Muruhuba beekūm (Hello to you)

How are you?

Greeting *Kayf haalak?* (How is your state [of health]?)
Kayf haalik (to a woman)
Reply *Al-humdoolillah, bikhair!* (Praise be to God, well!)

Note 1. *Al-humdoolillah,* means 'Praise be to God, I am well' and it is customary to say that you *are* even if you are at death's door! The reason is that by saying so the Muslim is acknowledging God's will over all things. (Later, if pressed, he might disclose more detail of his state of health.)

Note 2. The word *bikhair* is often omitted but understood.

And how are
you?

Greeting *Wa inta?* (*wa intee?* to a woman)
Reply *Al-humdoolillah, bikhair!* (Praise be to God, well!)

Goodbye

Greeting *Maa as-salaama* (With the peace [on you])
Reply *Maa as-salaama* or *Allah yisullmak* (God protect you) or *Fee amaan Allah* (To God's protection [I commit you])

Greeting	*Tisbah ala khair* (lit. May the morning find you well)	Goodnight
Reply	*Wa inta min ahal al-khair* or *wa inta min ahla*	

COMMON WORDS AND EXPRESSIONS

Yes	*Aiwa or na'aam*
No	*La*
Please	*Minfudluk*
Thank you	*Shūkraan* or *Mashkoor*
Thank you very much	*Shūkraan jazeelan*
That's all right	*Afwan*
Don't mention it	*La shūkraan ala waajib*
	(lit. Don't thank me, it is my duty)
What is your name please?	*Shoo ismak minfudlak?*

(There is no verb 'to be' in Arabic. *See* Basic Grammar below.)

My name is Mr Peters	*Ismee Meester Beeters*
Are you an American?	*Hal inta Amrikaanee?*
I am English	*Ana Ingleezee*
I am from England	*Ana min Ingletterra*
I am from America	*Ana min Amreeka*
I am French	*Ana Faransawi*
I am from France	*Ana min Faransa*
I'm pleased to meet you	*Tasharrufna* (lit. You honour me/us)
Do you speak Arabic?	*Tatakullum Arabee?* Or *Tahkee Arabee?*
Only a little	*Bass qaleel/shwei*
When will I see you?	*Aymta ashoofak?*
See you tomorrow	*Ashoofak būkra*
If God wills	*In-sha'Allah*
See you later	*Il al-liqqa* (lit: To the future)
How?	*Kayf?*
What?	*Shoo?* or *aysh?*
When?	*Aymta?*
Where?	*Wayn?* or *fayn?*
Why?	*Laysh?*
Who?	*Meen?*
And	*Wa*
Or	*Ow*

2

Thanks be to God	*Al-**hum**doolil**lah***
Good luck/best wishes	*Fūrsa saeeda* (lit. a happy occasion)
Excellent	*Mūmtaaz*
A little	*Qoleel* or *shwei*
Enough!	*Bass!*
Slowly/carefully please	*Shwei shwei min**fud**lak*
Be patient	*Khudh **baa**lak* or ***tow**wal **baa**lak*
Congratulations!	*Ma**brook**!* (lit. Blessed!)
Reply	*Allah yūbaarak feek* (lit. God bless you too)
Possibly/Maybe/Perhaps	***Yim**kin*
Good	***Teiy**yib* or *q**wai**yyis* (feminine: ***teiy**yiba* or *q**wai**yyisa*
No problem	*Mah fee **mūsh**killa*
Not good	*Mūsh **q**waiyyis(a)* or *mūsh **Teiy**yib(a)*
You are kind	***In**ta loteef*
I understand	*Af**ham***
I do not understand	*Ma af**ham***
What do you call this?	*Ma ism **haa**dha?*
What does this mean?	*Ma ma'ana **haa**dha?*
Never mind	***Ma**'alaysh* or *maa yūkhaalif*
I am sorry!	*Mūtta'**assif**!*
Excuse me	*Is**mah**lee*
Pardon/Excuse me	*Aasif*
Not at all/ Don't mention it	*Afwan*
I don't know	*Ana ma **aa**raf* or *ana ma **adree***
I didn't know	*Ana ma a**raft***
How far is it to...?	*Ma al-mas**aa**fa ila...?*

USEFUL PHRASES
At The Airport

My name is Peters	*Ismee **Bee**ters*
Do you speak English?	*Tata**kullam** Ing**lee**zee?*
Have you anything in your bag?	***Ein**dak shee fee ha**qeeb**tak?*

I have this (to declare) only	*Eindee haadha foqot/bass*
I have nothing (to declare)	*Ma eindee shee*
This is necessary for my work?	*Haadha dharooree li amalee/shoghallee*
Where is the toilet please?	*Wayn al-hamaam (al-twoylet) minfudlak?*
Where is the bank please?	*Wayn al-bank minfudlak?*
Where is my case?	*Wayn shantatee?*
Hi porter!	*Ya hammaal!*
This is mine / ours	*Haadha lee/ilna*
There is a case missing	*Naaqis shanta*
How much is that?	*Kam?*
Get me a taxi please	*Ūtlub lee taxi minfudlak*
I want to hire a car	*Ūreed astajir saiyaara*
Where is the bus to the city?	*Wayn al-buas lil madeena?*
Where is the British Consulate / Embassy?	*Wayn al-consuleeya/ As-sifaara al-Bareetaaneeya?*
I want to change some travellers cheques	*Ūreed ūsruf sheekaut seeyaheeya*

In a Taxi

Taxi!	*Taxi!*
To The Bustan Hotel please	*Il al-fūnduk al-Būstaan minfudlak*
Yes (Sir)	*Nu'am (seedee)*
How much?	*Kam?*
Twenty Riyals	*Ishreen riyaal*
No, that's a lot	*La, katheer*
Fifteen Riyals	*Khamsta'asher riyaal*
Good	*Teiyyib*
How many kilometres to the Hilton?	*Kam keeloomitr illal-Hiltoon*
Ten	*'ashara*
Go straight ahead	*Rūh mubaasharaton*
To the left here	*Il al-yesaar hina*
To the right	*Il al-yameen*
Stop there	*Woqqof hinaak*
Faster please	*Bisir'a minfudlak*
Slower please	*Bibbūt minfudlak*
Wait here please	*Intadhar hina minfudlak*

2

I will return in five minutes   *Aarja'baad* **kham***sa daqaa'iq*

In a Hotel

I have a reservation	*Eindee hajz*
I want a room please	*Ūreed ghūrfa minfudlak*
I want a double room	*Ūreed ghūrfa li*
with a bath	*shakhsayn laha hamaam*
Is there good air-conditioning?	*Hal al-mūkayyif teiyyib?*
How much is it a day?	*Kam al-eejaar li mūddat yome?*
(lit: How much is the rent	
for the period of a day?)	
Have you a cheaper room	*Eindak ghūrfa arkhas*
than that?	*min dhaalik?*
I want to see the room,	*Ūreed ashoof al-ghūrfa*
please	*minfudlak*
No, I don't like it	*La, maa ahibha*
Is there a better room?	*Fee ghūrfa ahsan?*
This is fine	*Haadha teiyyib*
Who is that?	*Meen?*
(to a knock at the door)	
A message for you	*Risaala lak*
A moment, please	*Lahdha, minfudlak*
Come in!	*Ta'aal!*
For you	*Illak*
Is there a reply?	*Fee jawaab?*

Calling on an Arab

Welcome	*Ahlan wa sahlan* (a shortened version is *ahlan*)
Replies	*Ahlan wa sahlan beek* or *feek* (to single host)
	Ahlan wa sahlan beekūm or *feekūm* (to more than one host)
I'd like to introduce Mr Peters	*Ahib ūqaddumlak Meester Beeters*
I'm pleased to meet you	*Tashurrufna* (lit: You honor us) or *Fūrsa saeeda* (lit: a happy occasion)

At this early stage, the greetings appropriate to the time of day will also be exchanged and enquiries made after each person's health (*see* p. 44)

Please sit down	*Minfudlak, astarreeh* or *tistarroh*
Reply	*Shūkraan* (Thank you)
Please have a cigarette?	*Tafuddal sigaara?*
Please have coffee / tea?	*Tafuddal qahwa/shei?*

Note 1: The meaning of the word *tafuddal* cannot be exactly translated into English. It is much used when offering or inviting someone politely to do or have something. Literally, it means 'be pleased to'.

You'll drink coffee / tea?	*Tishrub qahwa/shei?*
Reply	*Aiwa*

Note 2: Do not say 'thank you' as this is taken to mean 'no' in the same way that the French use 'merci'. It would, of course, be impolite to refuse refreshment. For further explanation *see* Chapter 3.

Enough, thank you	*Beekufee/bass, shūkraan*
That is enough [like that]	*Haadha kifaaya kida*
Delicious!	*Lodheedh!*

When you wish to say farewell you might say:

With your permission	*'an idhnak*

The host might then say:

You have honoured us	*Shurruftna*
Reply	*Tushurruft* (I have been honoured)
My home is your home	*Baytee baytak*
I compliment your cooking	*Tislam eedayk* (to a man) *eedaykee* (to a woman)

Shopping

The market	*As-sooq*

2

How much?	*Beekam?*
Eleven dinars	*Had'ashar denaar*
No, I'll give you five dinars	*La, aateek khamsa deenaar*
No, eight	*La, thamaania*
No, it is very expensive	*La, ghaalee jiddan*

(There is no exact Arabic translation for 'too' expensive)

Good (OK), seven dinars - my last word	*Teiyyib, saba'a deenaar aakhar kalaam*
OK, but it is expensive	*Teiyyib, laakin ghaalee*
No, it is cheap	*La, hūwa rakhees*
Is this shop open?	*Hal haadha ad-dūkkaan maftooh?*
No, it is closed [closed up]	*La, mūsakkar*
No it is closed [locked up]	*La, maqfool*
Do you want something?	*Tūreed Shee?*
No, I am only looking around	*La, atafarraj foqot*
Look! Look!	*Shoof! shoof!* (trader's shout)
A tip! A tip!	*Baqsheesh! baqsheesh!* (small boys' cry to tourists)

Replies:

I am in a rush	*Ana mūsta'jil* or
I have no change	*Maa eindee faqqar*
or I forgot, my wallet is in the hotel)	*Nasseet, al-mahjazza fil fūndūq*
or Run along! Run along!	*Imshee! Imshee!*
Where is the post office please?	*Wayn* (or *fayn*) *maktab al-bareed minfudlak?*
I want to buy (a shirt) please	*Ūreed ishteree (qomees) minfudlak*

Other words from the vocabulary can be substituted in this sentence.

Sightseeing

Where is the bus station please?	*Wayn mahattat al-baas minfudlak?*

(*al-Bass* or *as-Sayaara al-aam*, public car)

The first street on the left	*Awwal sharri'alal-yasaar*
Is it far from here?	*Ba'eed min hina?*
No, it is close. Only five minutes	*La, qoreeb. khamsa daqaa'iq foqot*
Is it possible to walk?	*Mūmkin imshee?*

Yes, it is (a distance of) 400 metres	*Aiwa, tab'ūd ala masaafa arba'a meeat meeter*
Where is the bus to Dubai?	*Wayn al-baas ila Dubai?*
How much?	*Beekam?*
Tell me when we arrive please	*Qullee eind al-wusool minfudlak*
Where are we now?	*Wayn nehnaa alaan?*
When do we go?	*Aymta nimshee?*
After ten minutes	*Ba'ad 'ashara daqaa'iq*
Where is the best place to go?	*Wayn ahsan makaan arooh?*
Yes, come!	*Aiwa, ta'aal!*
What is there here?	*Shoo hinaak?*
Taxi! Do you know where the office of tourism is?	*Taxi! ta'rif wayn maktab as-seeyaaha?*
I want to visit (the museum)	*Ūreed azoor (al-mat'haf)*

Eating Out

Is there a cafe near here?	*Fee maqha qoreeb min hina?*
A cold lemon drink please	*Laymoon baarid minfudlak*
Tea / coffee please	*Shei/qahwa minfudlak*
How many do you want?	*Kam tūreed?*
For how many people?	*Li kam nafar?*
Two please	*Ithnayn minfudlak*
Have you got Nescafe?	*Eindak qahwa neskafay?*
With milk and sugar	*Maa haleeb wa sookar*
The bill please	*Al-hisaab minfudlak*
Is there a restaurant near here?	*Fee mattam qoreeb min hina?*
Please, we would like (kebabs)	*Minfudlak nūreed (kabaab)*

Miscellaneous Phrases

Is it possible to play (tennis) here?	*Mūmkin al'ab (tennees) hina?*
Is there a swimming pool?	*Fee hammaam sabaaha?*
I want to swim in the sea	*Ūreed asbah fil bahr*
Is it possible to fish here?	*Mūmkin sayd as-samak hina?*
[Reply] Of course, certainly!	*Ma'loom!*
Is there (a barber) here, please?	*Fee (hallaaq) hina, minfudlak?*

2

EMERGENCY PHRASES

Call the Police!	*Ūtlub al-boolees!*
Call An Ambulance!	*Ūtlub al-is'aaf!*
Call the Fire Brigade!	*Ūtlub al-mataafee!* or *Itfaa'eeya*
Call a Doctor!	*Ūtlub al-doctoor!*
Careful (Take it easy)	*Ala mahlak*
Careful! (A hole in the road)	*Ihtaris!*
Careful! (Pay attention)	*Khūdh baalak!*
Come here!	*Ta'aal!* (pl. *ta'aaloo*)
Danger	*Khatar*
Take it easy!	*Tawwel baalak!*
Help!/Rescue me!	*An-najda!*
Fire!	*Hareeq!*
Go away!	*Insarif!*
I'm ill	*Ana mareed*
I've lost my way	*Ana tūht*
Leave me alone!	*Itrūkni li-haali!* (said with conviction)
Or if you don't, I'll call the police	*Wa illa la, ajeeblak al-boolees*
Listen!	*Isma'!*
Look	*Ūnzūr* or *shoof!*
Quickly	*Bi sir'a*
Stop!	*Qiff!* (or *Woqqof*)
Stop that man!	*Amsik haadha ar-rajūl!*
Thief!	*Liss!*
Is it important?	*Hoowa mūhim?*
Is it urgent?	*Haadha musta'jil?*

Telling the Time

What is the time please?	*As-saa'a kam minfudlak?*
Five minutes past twelve	*As-saa'a ithna'ashar wa khamsa daqaa'iq*

Arabs say 'The hour [is] twelve and five minutes'. This is the same for all times except quarter past, twenty past, and half past.

Quarter past twelve	*As-saa'a ithna'ashar wa ruba'* (lit: twelve and a quarter)

2

Twenty past twelve	*As-saa'a ithna'ashar wa thūlth* (lit: twelve and a third)
Half past twelve	*As-saa'a ithna'ashar wa nuss* (lit: twelve and a half)
Twenty to one	*As-saa'a waahida ila thūlth* (lit: one less a third)
Quarter to one	*As-saa'a waahida ila ruba'* (lit: one less a quarter)
Five to one	*As-saa'a waahida ila khamsa* (lit: one less five)
One o'clock	*As-saa'a waahida*

BASIC GRAMMAR

Although Arabic as a Semitic language is structurally different from English, it is in many ways simpler. Firstly, it is phonetic – a word is pronounced as it is written and there are no silent letters. Secondly, the rules of grammar tend to be obeyed whereas in English there are many exceptions. Finally, although it looks complicated, the script has a rational basis with only a few more letters and sounds than in English.

Tri-literal Roots

In common with all Semitic languages, most Arabic words can be traced back to a three- or sometimes four-consonant root which is normally a verb. For example, the consonant **K** plus **T** plus **B** is the root for 'writing'. By putting vowels and other consonants around this root in various combinations, it is possible to make up all the words to do with writing:

KaTaB	=	he wrote
KaTaBoo	=	they wrote
ya**KTaB**	=	he will write
KiTaaB	=	a book
KaaTiB	=	a clerk
ma**KTaB**	=	an office
ma**KTaBa**	=	a library
ma**KTooB**	=	it is written

2

Word Order

The word order in a sentence of literary Arabic is *verb, subject, object*. In the spoken language, however, the order is as in English – *subject, verb and object*.

Numbers

Arabic numbers as figures and in spoken form are given below:

0	.	*sifr*	10	١٠	**ashara**
1	١	**waahid**	11	١١	**hada'shar**
2	٢	**ithnayn**	12	١٢	**ithna'ashar**
3	٣	**thalaatha**	13	١٣	**thalaathtat'ashar**
4	٤	**arba'a**	14	١٤	**arbat'ashar**
5	٥	**khamsa**	15	١٥	khamst'ashar
6	٦	**sitta**	16	١٦	**sitt'ashar**
7	٧	**saba'a**	17	١٧	saba'at'ashar
8	٨	**thamaania**	18	١٨	**thamaant'tashar**
9	٩	**tis'a**	19	١٩	**tis'at'ashar**

20	٢٠	**'ishreen**
21	٢١	**waahid wa 'Ishreen**
30	٣٠	**thalaatheen**
40	٤٠	**arba'een**
50	٥٠	**khamseen**
60	٦٠	**sitteen**
70	٧٠	**saba'een**
80	٨٠	**thamaanee'een**
90	٩٠	**tis'een**
100	١٠٠	**meea**

Numbers after 20 are made up on the following pattern:

22	٢٢	*ithnayn wa 'ishreen*
33	٣٣	*thalaatha wa thalaatheen*
48	٤٨	*thamaania wa arba'een*

2

Unlike words or sentences, numbers in Arabic are written from left to right, i.e. 2005 = ٢٠٠٥. However, groups of numbers such as dates are usually written so that the groups themselves run from right to left, i.e. 21/5/2005 = ٢٠٠٥/٥/٢١ .

A or An

There is no indefinite article (a/an) in Arabic and it is unnecessary to qualify a single object by using *waahid* (one). For example, *wulud* (boy), when standing on its own, means 'a' or 'one' boy.

Two

There is a special way of saying 'two' of anything in Arabic. this is know as the 'dual' and is formed by adding the ending *ayn* to the noun e.g. *wulud* means 'one boy' *wuludayn* means 'two boys'. If the noun ends in 'a', add '*tayn*' to it, e.g. *ghurfatayn* = two rooms.

Numbers 3 to 10

From 3 to 10 the accompanying noun is in the plural but from eleven onwards it is in the singular, e.g.

thalaatha awlaad	three boys (*awlaad* is the plural of *wulud*)
'ishreen wulud	twenty boys

Percentages

Ten per cent is rendered as 'ten in (a) hundred' e.g.

ashara bil meea

Twenty per cent is *'ishreen bil meea*

Fractions

The basic fractions which you might need are:

a half	*nūss*
a quarter	*ruba'*
a third	*thūlth*

The Definite Article

This is *Al* in Arabic. In spoken Arabic, in front of words beginning with *t th d dh s sh r z n* and sometimes *g*, the *l*

2

of the article is assimilated. So *al-shams* (the sun) is pronounced *ash-shams*.

Nouns

Nouns in Arabic are either masculine or feminine in gender. Nouns referring only to females may be assumed to be feminine and so may most nouns ending in *a*. Most other nouns will be masculine – there are exceptions, of course, and these simply need to be learnt, as the adjective must always agree with its noun.

Plurals

As explained above, there are three kinds of quantity in Arabic – the singular, the dual and the plural. Plurals are formed in two ways. They are either broken plurals or sound plurals. The broken plurals are not formed on one particular pattern but are nevertheless variants of the singular and are best learnt by rote. For example:

Singular   *wulud* (boy)   Plural *aw**laad*** (boys)
Singular   *bayt* (house)   Plural *boo**yoot*** (houses)

Sound plurals if they are feminine and end in *a* form the plural by adding *aat*:

Singular   *hu**koo**ma* (government)
Plural   *hukoo**maat*** (governments)

and masculine nouns referring to people form their plural simply by adding *een*:

Singular   ***Mus**lim*
Plural   *Musli**meen***

Adjectives

Adjectives follow their noun. If the noun carries the definite article then so does the adjective, e.g.
*al-wulud <u>al</u>-sa**gheer*** = The small boy

2

Normally adjectives agree with the noun in gender and number. However, when the noun is referring to plural 'things' or 'animals' then the adjective is put in the feminine singular by adding the suffix *a*, e.g.

as-sanawaat al-akheera = the recent years

The comparative of most adjectives takes the following form:

kabeer = big	and	*akbar* = bigger
rakhees = cheap	and	*arkhas* = cheaper
katheer = many	and	*akthar* = more

Verbs

Arabic has only two tenses – one denoting completed action, and the other incomplete action. In simple terms this means a past tense and a present tense. The present tense is also used to cover the future. For example:

katab = he wrote (past)
yaktūb = he is writing (present) or he will write (future)

The verb 'to be' does not exist in the present tense. For example:

al-wulud sagheer = the boy is small ('is' being understood)

In colloquial Arabic, 'there is' and 'there are' are translated by the word *fee*, followed by the noun in the singular or plural:

fee hallaaq hina = there is a barber here
fee booyoot hinaak? = are there houses there?

'There was' and 'there were' are translated by the words *kaan fee*.

he was = *kaan*　　she was = **kaanat**　　I was = *kūnt*
he will be =*yakoon*　she will be =*takoon*　I will be = **akoon**

2

Simple regular verbs in Arabic consist of a root of three consonants and when an Arab refers to a verb he uses the third person singular:

katab = he wrote (i.e. to write – there is no infinitive in Arabic)

The Past Tense

This is formed by attaching suffixes to the root *katab*.

*kat**abt***	I wrote	*katab**na***	we wrote
*kat**abt***	you (masc.) wrote	*katab**too***	you (pl.) wrote
*kat**abtee***	you (fem.) wrote	*katab**oo***	they wrote
katab	he wrote		
***kat**abat*	she wrote		

Note that the subject pronoun (I, you, he etc.) is normally omitted in Arabic.

The Present and Future Tense

This is formed with a prefix (and sometimes also a suffix) to the modified root and by changing its second vowel:

***a**ktūb*	I write	***na**ktūb*	we write
***ta**ktūb*	you (masc.) write	***ta**ktūboo*	you (pl.) write
***ta**ktūbee*	you (fem.) write	***ya**ktūboo*	they write
***ya**ktūb*	he writes		
***ta**ktūb*	she writes		

Although the final vowel change varies and must be learnt for each verb, the same format is used for most regular verbs.

The Imperative

This is formed on the following pattern:

Singular	***Ū**ktūb!*	write!
Plural	***Ū**ktūboo!*	write!

The Negative

This is formed by putting *maa* in front of the verb:

Maa katabt   I did not write

In sentences without the verb 'to be', the word *mush* is used:

Ana mush min London I am not from London

The imperative is negated by prefixing *laa* to the present tense:

Laa tūktūb!   don't write!

Personal Pronouns

These are as follows:

ana	I	*nehna*	we
inta	you (masc.)	*intūm*	you (pl.)
intee	you (fem.)	*hūm*	they
hoowa	he/it		
heeya	she/it		

Possession and Object of a Verb

This is denoted by attaching suffixes to the noun:

-ee	my	*-na*	ours
-ak	yours (masc.)	*-kūm*	yours(pl.)
-ik	yours (fem.)	*-hūm*	theirs
-oh	his		
-ha	hers		

e.g. *bayt* + *ee* = my house

When a noun has a feminine ending *a*, then *t* is put in front of the suffix:

seiyaara = car,   and   *seiyaaratee* = my car
e.g. *seiyaara* + *t* + *ee*

2

The object of a verb is also denoted by using the same suffix, with the exception that *ee* becomes *nee*:
he struck me = *darubnee*

To have

This is expressed in Arabic by adding the same suffixes to the word *eind*. For example:

eindee = I have   *eindak* = you have

But there is a Special Rule of Possession in Arabic called the construct state: 'The house of the boy' is not translated as such. In Arabic this would be:

bayt al-wulud = (the) house (of) the boy

The definite article is dropped from the first word and 'of' is understood. Names are considered definite and so:

bayt Mohammed = Mohammed's house

Questions

To ask a question, use the same intonation as in English: alternatively, preface the sentence with *'hal'*.

Eindak qahwa?/Hal eindak qahwa? = have you (got) coffee?

There is much more to Arabic grammar, but it is hoped that these simplified rules will be a helpful introduction.

THE ARABIC SCRIPT

One of the reasons people consider Arabic a difficult language is the complicated appearance of the script. But it is not that difficult if you analyse it.*
    Arabic script is written from right to left and is cursive, i.e. most of the letters in any word are joined together.

* *See* James Peters' *Very Simple Arabic Script*

2

The twenty-nine characters of the Arabic alphabet are given below. Most have an equivalent sound in English. There are no capital letters in Arabic. Each letter has a slightly different form depending on its position in a word, but its basic characteristic is always recognisable:

Name of letter	Pronunciation	End	Middle	Beginning
ا *alif*	a as in apple	ا	ا	أ
ب *ba*	b as in ball	ـب	ـبـ	بـ
ت *ta*	t as in top	ـت	ـتـ	تـ
ث *tha*	th as in thin	ـث	ـثـ	ثـ
ج *jeem*	j as in job	ـج	ـجـ	جـ
ح *ha* (hard)	h as in hoot	ـح	ـحـ	حـ
خ *kha*	kh as in loch	ـخ	ـخـ	خـ
د *daal*	d as in day	ـد	ـلـ	د
ذ *dhaal*	th as in then	ـذ	ـذـ	ذ
ر *ra*	r rolled as in roar	ـر	ـر	ر
ز *za*	z as in zebra	ـز	ـز	ز
س *seen*	s as in sit	ـس	ـسـ	سـ
ش *sheen*	sh as in shine	ـش	ـشـ	شـ
ص *sawd*	s as in sword, said with emphasis	ـص	ـصـ	صـ
ض *dawd*	d as in door, said with emphasis	ـض	ـضـ	ضـ
ط *to*	t as in taught, said with emphasis	ـط	ـطـ	طـ
ظ *dho*	th as in then, said with emphasis	ـظ	ـظـ	ظـ
ع *'ein*	like a glottal stop	ـع	ـعـ	عـ
غ *ghein*	like the r in French 'rue'	ـغ	ـغـ	غـ
ف *fa*	f as in feed	ـف	ـفـ	فـ
ق *qaaf*	c as in caught or in some countries a glottal stop	ـق	ـقـ	قـ
ك *kaf*	k as in kite	ـك	ـكـ	كـ
ل *lam*	l as in let	ـل	ـلـ	لـ
م *meem*	m as in met	ـم	ـمـ	مـ

2

Name of letter	Pronunciation	Form depending on position		
		End	Middle	Beginning
ن noon	n as in net	ن	ـنـ	نـ
ه ha(soft)	h as in hear	ـه	ـهـ	هـ
و wow	w as in well	ـو	ـو	و
ي ya	y as in yet	ـي	ـيـ	يـ
ء hamza	glottal stop (gentler than the 'ein)			

Short Vowels

There are three short vowels which are sounded but are normally omitted in writing. Exceptions are the Holy Quran and in calligraphy.

ـَ written above the word, sounds like the 'a' in pat

ـِ written below the word, sounds like the 'i' in pit

ـُ written above the word, sounds like short 'u' in put

Long Vowels

These are formed by following a short vowel with the letter associated with it (reading right to left):

اَ sounds like an 'a' in pass (short 'a' plus an *alif*)

وُ sounds like an 'oo' in root (short 'u' plus *wow*)

يِ sounds like an 'ee' in feet (short 'i' plus *ya*)

Diphthongs

These are formed by combining short and long vowels:

وَ sounds like 'ow' in cow (short 'a' plus *wow*)

يَ sounds like 'ay' in 'hay' (short 'a' plus *ya*)

2

Dots

These are often joined in handwriting:

ت handwritten looks like   ـتـ

ث handwritten looks like   ـثـ

Special 'a'

In some cases the ى without the dots at the end of a word is pronounced as a long 'a' sound. These have to be learnt by experience.

Ta marboota

The letter ة or ه is often found at the end of a word with two dots above it: i.e. ة This is a common form of feminine ending. It is usually pronounced as an 'a' sound. When followed by the definite article it is pronounced as a 't'. It is called a *ta marboota*.

Orthographic Signs

The most common are:

ْ   used to mark a consonant without a vowel

ً   at the end of a word, giving the sound 'an'

ّ   above a letter, has the effect of doubling it

آ   when two long 'a's follow each other, one is written horizontally above the other

Examples

By referring to the alphabet it should be possible to decipher the following words. (Remember to read from right to left.)

ك + ت + ب = كَتَب   spells *katab* and means 'he wrote'

ا+ل+ب+ي+ت = أَلْبَيْت spells *al-bayt* and means 'the house'

هـ + د + ف = هَدَف   spells *hadaf* and means 'target'

Examples of Common Signs

مَطَار	Airport	خَطَر المَوْت	Mortal danger
إسْعَاف	Ambulance	بَلَدِيَّة	Municipality
أَلْقَادِمُون	Arrivals	مَتْحَف	Museum
مَصْرِف/بَنْك	Bank	مَمْنُوع الدُّخُول	No entry
حَلَّاق	Barber	مَمْنُوع الوُقُوف	No parking
مَكْتَبَة	Bookshop	مَمْنُوع التَصْوير	No photography
مَكْتَب ٱلصَّرَّاف	Bureau de Change	مَمْنُوع التَدْخين	No smoking
		قَصْر	Palace
مَقْهَى	Café	جَوَاز سَفَر	Passports
مَرْكَز لِ...	Centre (for)	شُرْطَة	Police
شَرَكَة	Company	مَخْفَر الشُرْطَة	Police station
قُنْصُلِيَّة	Consulate	ميناء	Port
جُمْرُك	Customs	خَاصْ	Private
خَطَرا!	Danger!	إسْحَب	Pull
أَلمُغَادِرُون	Departures	إدْفَع	Push
مَدْخَل	Entrance	مَطْعَم	Restaurant
مَعْرَض	Exhibition	مَدْرَسَة	School
مَخْرَج	Exit	قِفْ!	Stop!
مطْفَأَة حَريق	Fire extinguisher	خَيَّاط	Tailor
مَمْنُوع	Forbidden	تَكْسي للإجْرَة	Taxi (sign for hire)
مُسْتَشْفَى	Hospital	تَلفُون	Telephone
فُنْدُق	Hotel	دَوْرَة المِياه/حَمَّام	Toilet
مَصْعَد	Lift	رِجَال/سَيِّدَات	Men/Women
ثَكْنَة/مُعَسْكَر	Military camp	جَامِعَة	University

Note: The Arabic would usually be without short vowels.

CHAPTER THREE

Etiquette

INTRODUCTION

There is a strict code of social conduct or etiquette throughout the Peninsula and it is possible for a foreigner who is ignorant of it to give offence, although it must be said that the Arabs are generally very tolerant of foreigners who are clearly unaware of it. Arab courtesy is such that even if someone does transgress they must never be allowed to know it. Nevertheless, it is a decided advantage to understand the basic rules, and the purpose of this chapter is to explain the key common denominators of etiquette pertaining to the region as a whole. Once you understand them do not be over-confident. Some of the worst howlers are committed by those with a little knowledge who imagine they can extrapolate from it to meet an unfamiliar situation. Only practise what you know to be correct.

ARAB COURTESY

No visitor to the Arabian Peninsula can fail to be impressed by the friendliness, courtesy and unfailing hospitality of the Arabs and the most important characteristic for personal success is to be well-mannered. As Sir Donald Hawley writes in his book *Manners and Correct Form in the Middle East*, 'The ill-mannered man is not forgiven, and, however well-intentioned he may be, he will fail.' The best advice to someone visiting the region is to be polite, patient and as considerate as the Arabs are themselves.

CALLING ON AN ARAB

The Arab Perception of Time
The first hurdle in a foreigner's understanding is likely to be the Arab perception of time. It is quite different to that in the West. One should always be on time for any

Appointments

appointment but be prepared to wait, sometimes for a long time, or even to have a meeting postponed or conceivably cancelled. On the occasions when this happens it is not necessarily bad manners or forgetfulness but of necessity. The person you are visiting will have acted for reasons which may not seem justified to you but which are perfectly valid in his culture. His presence may have been requested at short notice by a more senior person or for important family business. You should resist the inclination to feel frustrated or slighted and accept the situation with good grace. As you become more familiar with the culture you will begin to understand.

Shaking Hands

Shaking
hands

Whenever you greet or take leave of someone always shake hands and only with the right hand. Try not to use too firm a grip. On entering a room full of people, shake hands and exchange greetings first with the person on whom you are calling and then with as many others present as seems appropriate, i.e. those in the immediate vicinity of your host. It is customary to shake hands even if you have not been formally introduced. Once an Arab feels he knows you do not be surprised if he holds on to your hand as a mark of friendship or occasionally taps you on the arm during conversation to emphasis a point. Arabs are more tactile than Westerners. *See also* Chapter 1 – *Values.*

One exception to the rule of shaking hands is that it is not normal for a man to shake the hand of an Arab woman unless she follows the Western custom and specifically offers it.

Greetings

It is particularly important to give a person on whom you are calling his correct name and title. Detailed advice on Arab names and forms of address are given later in this Chapter under *Forms of Address.* Although Arabs are only too conscious of the difficulties of their language and will almost certainly greet you in English, you may sometimes gain enormous kudos if you are able to master one or two of the basic pleasantries in Arabic. The standard greetings are given in Chapter 2 , but the most common general greeting in the Peninsula is:

Greeting	*As-salaam alaykum*
	(Peace be on you)
Reply	*Wa alaykum as-salaam*
	(And on you be peace)

An Arab may also say to you	*Ahlan wa sahlan!*
	(Welcome!)
To which the reply is	*Ahlan wa sahlan beekūm!*
	(And to you!)

Enquiries are then always made into each other's health; a formula which is invariably observed no matter how frequently you meet someone or talk on the phone. Even if you ring an Arab say, twice in one hour it is still considered important to ask how he is before mentioning the subject of your call. When you get to know an Arab better, you might also ask after the well-being of his family. Enquiries about the family are restricted to the collective family and children. Because of the greater privacy accorded to women in the Arab world one should never enquire after an Arab's wife, unless you or your wife know the family very well.

Taking a Seat

When you enter the office of an Arab for a business meeting do not be surprised to find it full of other visitors. A senior Arab figure will routinely receive large numbers of people each day who may call to enlist his help or simply to greet him. When you introduce yourself to your host you should, unless it seems inappropriate, give him your card. If you intend to be a regular visitor to the region this should be printed in Arabic as well as English.

A seat will then be indicated to you, possibly with the word *tafuddal (see below)*.

tafuddal

Tafuddal

The meaning of this word cannot be exactly translated into English but is the term used when offering a seat or ushering someone through a doorway. Literally translated it means 'be pleased to' or 'be so good as to' (go first). If the room is crowded the seat will probably be on the immediate right or left of your host and this position is usually reserved for the most important visitor. In other words, because you are the latest arrival you are considered most important – for the moment anyway. When someone else arrives you should stand up, shake hands with the newcomer and be prepared to vacate your seat for him. Watch your host and take your lead from him.

The Sole of the Foot

A traditional custom in the Arab world which is still observed today is to avoid presenting the sole of your foot directly at another person. The sole of the foot was traditionally considered unclean and this used to mean, and still does in some countries, that you are intentionally insulting that person. So to be on the safe side it is advisable to sit with both feet on the floor and not cross your legs unless your host does so and even then to avoid presenting your sole directly to him. If you are fortunate enough to be invited to an Arab meal sitting on the floor the same rule applies. Shoes are removed and the soles of the feet tucked in underneath or kept behind you.

Refreshments

When you visit an Arab he will invariably offer you refreshment, normally tea or coffee, and it is usual to wait for this to arrive before mentioning the purpose of your visit. However, it is becoming increasingly common in some circles to dispense with such formalities and start talking seriously as soon as greetings have been exchanged. Your host's manner and general comportment will usually tell you what type of person he is. If he abides by the traditional

Arabic coffee

3

custom, the initial greetings will be followed by a period of silence or confined to general enquiries after your well-being or journey until a servant enters with tea or coffee.

You can be offered a variety of refreshments. In many places in the region you will still be offered Arab coffee (*qahwa*) in the Bedu tradition. It would be impolite to refuse. Arab coffee is pale, bitter and often flavoured with cardamon and other spices. A small amount is poured from a long spouted brass coffee pot into a small handleless cup which should be taken in the right hand, even if you are left-handed. Only the right hand should be used when drinking, eating, smoking or offering anything to another person (even for waving in welcome). Drink as many cups as you like but not a lot more than your host or others present. Two or three is usual.

The signal to show that you have had enough is to give the cup a quick twist or shake when handing it back. If it is handed back without doing this the server will simply continue to refill it. It is not done to *say* that you have had sufficient – just indicate by shaking the cup. You may also be offered dates with the coffee. You could also be offered thick, strong, Turkish coffee (in a small cup) after being asked whether you take it without sugar, medium or sweet but this is a custom more common to the Levant and other Arab countries outside the Gulf region. It may be accompanied by a glass of water to quench the thirst. Turkish coffee should be sipped, being careful to leave the thick coffee grounds in the bottom of the cup. Another refreshment offered is tea in the Arab style which is sweet, without milk and served in a small glass cup and saucer

These are the most common refreshments but it is becoming increasingly common in large establishments with perhaps a lot of expatriate employees, to serve instant coffee and tea or a soft drink or a glass of water.

Smoking is becoming less popular in the Middle East, as elsewhere, and one should only smoke if invited to do so, or following the host's lead.

Shaking the coffee cup

71

Broaching the Subject of Your Visit

Generally speaking, once refreshments have been served, the moment should be opportune for you to consider raising the subject of your visit. However, it is usually best to wait until you are invited to do so or to have a clear sign from your host that he is willing for it to be introduced. You must be particularly sensitive to the mood and circumstances of the meeting and not force the pace. Give your host long enough and he will normally give you an indication. The last thing you should do is to show impatience. In the event that you are clearly discouraged from talking seriously, do not be tempted to persist. There is likely to be a good reason. You should also avoid discussing your business in front of others. Simply ask if you can meet again.

Never expect a topic to be raised, discussed and a decision taken on your first visit. An Arab will not only wish to get to know you, but also consider the matter you are bringing to his attention; it would be quite wrong to push him just because your time is limited. It should be his concept of time that matters rather than yours.

Communication

As has been said, many Arabs speak good English. Nevertheless, as a general rule you should bear the following points in mind:

Make due allowance for a limited knowledge of English. A limited vocabulary may make a person's meaning obscure. If you are in any doubt it is prudent to rephrase it back to him diplomatically to confirm. The limited command of a language can also make a phrase sound unintentionally rude. An example of this can be seen when a customs official at the airport says to you 'Give passport!' because those are the only words he knows in English.

Use simple English. Native English speakers use the vernacular without thinking and it can be particularly difficult to understand if English is not your mother

Getting to the point

Plain English

tongue. Use short sentences rather than long ones for additional clarity.

Make your point briefly and succinctly. When the opportunity arises to mention the subject of your visit, for example a business proposal, do not wrap it up with a long lead in or a detailed explanation. At an initial meeting a brief and succinct description is far more likely to elicit interest and hopefully, the dialogue will proceed from there.

Avoid discussing politics, religion and women. Suffice it to say that these are delicate and often emotive subjects. Refer to the Gulf and not the Persian Gulf (*see* Chapter 1 – *Historical Summary*). Respect Islam but don't be tempted to comment on it. Finally, women in the Arab world enjoy an altogether more secluded position than in many other cultures and a male visitor should avoid mentioning them. Asking an Arab if he has children on the other hand can open a topic of genuine mutual interest.

Conversational Faux Pas

Be careful with humour. Arabs have a great sense of fun. Do not be afraid to show that you have a sense of

THE ARAB SENSE OF HUMOUR

There is an old story of a ruling Arab Sheikh who, in the early days of the development of the Peninsula states, asked a British official to send him an 'expert'. The British offical readily agreed but asked what the expert's specialisation was to be. The Sheikh replied that he did not want the official to invent problems, just to provide him with an expert. 'Right, Your Highness!' said the British official and took his leave. As he reached the door, the Sheikh called out, 'And another thing, let him have only one arm.' 'Only one arm, Your Highness?' queried the official. 'Yes,' said the Sheikh, 'I want none of this, "on the one hand . . . and on the other hand"!'

3

humour but do not attempt to entertain an Arab with jokes until you are quite sure what he does or does not appreciate. Never use sarcasm or irony. It is likely to be misunderstood or regarded as unkind.

Do not worry about pauses in conversation. Silences are not embarrassing to an Arab. He does not feel the need as we do to maintain a steady flow of conversation. Indeed, lengthy silences are often the norm in Arab social gatherings. They will often simply take pleasure in each other's company.

Be diplomatic. Nothing you say or do must in any way be construed as critical, disapproving or patronising about the Arab world.

In short, be careful what you say. Avoid going to extremes. Don't bore your host with the merits of your own country, government or systems. He may take it as implying criticism of his own. You should aim to demonstrate that you are a straightforward and discreet person with balanced personal views, whom he can trust.

Interruptions
You may be fortunate in being alone with your host but you should not be thrown if there are others present and the meeting is subject to interruptions. Because of the open-door policy of the Arab culture anyone, particularly an important person, may call on your host at any time and each new arrival will receive the same courteous welcome as yourself. The telephone or an intercom may also interrupt the dialogue. Having said that, an Arab appreciates privacy as much as you do and if he likes you, the initial contact usually leads to a private meeting. But it is your host who will determine that. You may hint that you have something confidential or important to impart and even invite him for a private meal in a restaurant or hotel but usually it is he who will make the first steps towards meeting in a more private venue.

Open door
policy

Personal Relationships

As emphasised in Chapter 1, the Arabs set great store by personal relationships. You will always be greeted courteously but beyond that you may or may not detect that an Arab is holding back until he is clear what sort of person you are, if he considers he can trust you or if he is interested in conducting business with you. Your demeanour must be open, friendly and polite but not over-familiar or ingratiating. A relationship of trust on both sides will take time to establish. As a general rule, the degree of mutual trust will be commensurate with the number of times you have met.

Rapport

3

Cancelled Meetings

As mentioned earlier, do not show any sign of annoyance or frustration if a meeting is cancelled or interrupted, when, for example, your host's presence is demanded elsewhere, sometimes at short notice. Practical difficulties and misunderstandings do occur. In order to succeed one must be able to accept such situations with equanimity, however inconvenient, demonstrating a calm and relaxed attitude. See *The Arab Perception of Time* above.

Taking Your Leave

Initial visits are usually short. Do not attempt to achieve significant results at a first meeting. It is quite enough to introduce yourself and perhaps the subject of your visit. Overstaying your welcome could jeopardise your chances later on. If you are a businessman, you might leave a brochure or briefing document with your card. On leaving, if possible remember the phrase for 'Goodbye':

Farewells

Greeting   *Maa as-salaama* (lit. With the peace [on you])
Reply   *Maa as-salaama* or *Allah yisullmak* (God
                protect you)

If, on leaving an office or Arab house, your host escorts you to the door he will invariably stand on your left and

75

invite you to go through the door first, usually with the word *Tafuddal*. It is considered polite to demur once or twice before accepting. The reverse would apply if you were the host and then your guest would politely refuse once or twice before accepting.

RECEIVING AN ARAB

When receiving an Arab in your own office or home country, extend him all of the foregoing courtesies in return:

♦ A warm welcome, handshake and seating
♦ Enquiries after his health, general wellbeing and exchange of pleasantries
♦ Encouragement to raise the subject of his visit, unless it is a social call, but without undue haste
♦ Offer further hospitality if appropriate – e.g. if he is visiting for a period of time
♦ On departure, escort him to the front door of your premises and to his car

ENTERTAINMENT

A Meal in An Arab House

A visitor may be fortunate enough to be invited to an Arab meal or party (*hufla*). Invitations are very often issued at short notice.

Arrive shortly after the time on the invitation and dress in a suit and tie or open-necked shirt depending on the circumstances. One should get local advice on what is appropriate. Most parties to which businessmen are invited are all-male affairs. However, if, exceptionally, it is the sort of party where wives are included, then it may be polite to take a bouquet of flowers for the hostess. Again, take local advice.

Party introductions

On arrival, the guests are ushered into a reception room where the host will introduce them to those already present, starting with the most important. If the party is a family affair then family elders will come into this category and a foreign visitor should show them due deference and attention. It is the general custom to remove one's shoes, either on arrival or, if the meal is to be eaten at floor level, certainly on entry to the dining room. Follow the lead of your host.

After a period for liquid refreshment the guests are shown into the dining room where the meal will be set out either on tables or at floor level. Meals served at table usually follow the general international pattern, i.e. soup, followed by a main course and then a variety of sweetmeats or fruit. A good host will ply you with more and more food, and it is the custom to leave a little food on your plate to indicate that you have had enough. If the meal is served on the floor be careful not to present the soles of your feet to other people. If the meal is eaten in the traditional way there will be no knives or forks except perhaps for a knife which the host or a helper will use to cut meat from a joint or carcass. Use only the right hand for eating. Some people sit on their left hand as a reminder! The main course is generally rice with chicken or lamb. The host will sometimes offer a tender piece of meat or fruit to a guest and this should be politely accepted although, since all etiquette is exaggerated, some guests may out of politeness refuse before accepting. (A simple refusal is often not taken at face value.) Contrary to popular Western belief, sheep's eyes are not considered a delicacy.

Traditional meals

When the meal is over, the guests wash their hands and return to the reception room where coffee and possibly more sweetmeats or dates are served. Incense is often brought round at this point. It is polite to take your leave shortly after drinking coffee, and certainly after the incense. Your host may at some point invite you to smoke a *nargeela* (hubble-bubble). This has a long pipe and the smoker draws the tobacco smoke through scented water.

The hubble-bubble

Formal Receptions

These are an increasingly common feature in the modern official and business life of the Peninsula. Foreigners normally wear a suit. Receptions are usually held in the

3

early evening and last for a couple of hours. The period is sometimes stipulated on the invitation, eg. 6 to 8pm. One should arrive fairly promptly, five or ten minutes after the time on the invitation. The host and his colleagues usually position themselves near the entrance to the reception room and greet the guests on arrival. Snacks or a buffet will be available at side tables or brought round by waiters. Again, only use the right hand for drinking, eating and smoking. Wives and other ladies may be present at this sort of function but often form a group among themselves. It is better to avoid engaging an Arab wife in conversation alone. At the appropriate hour the guests take their leave, saying farewell to the host and other dignitaries positioned at the entrance.

As well as giving the usual greeting, you might congratulate your Arab host if the party is being given to mark a special occasion, such as a National Day. The appropriate Arabic word is *Mabrook*! (Congratulations!).

Entertaining in a Peninsula Country

Entertaining

The majority of entertainment arranged by foreign visitors in the region is in the form of the formal reception above or a meal in a restaurant or hotel. Sometimes functions are held on a motorised dhow which should have toilet facilities and adequate protection from the weather. All of these venues have the added advantage that the local hotel manager is likely to be well versed in the correct form for such occasions.

Any party should be in keeping with local custom i.e. sexes should be segregated, pork products should not be served and a careful decision whether to serve alcohol should be made. A Muslim is forbidden by the laws of Islam to eat pork or drink alcohol and all meat must be *halaal*, i.e. permitted and slaughtered in the prescribed manner.

Invitations

For formal functions an invitation card should be produced in English and, in certain circumstances, in Arabic as well. Local advice should be sought on what is appropriate. An Arabic card can be produced in the country concerned, or by one of the many good Arabic printers in the West. The more important the function, the more elaborate the card. It would usually include the company logo.

The guest list should be completed with care to ensure the inclusion of the correct levels and numbers for your purpose. It is always best to seek informed advice on any guest list, and the embassy or local adviser can usually help. A high ranking Arab will be particular about who else is attending the function and his secretary will often ring the host to find out. Invitations are not always acknowledged and you should not read any special significance into non-attendance.

In the more conservative states, Arab women may not as a rule attend mixed functions unless they are private family affairs and the hosts are close friends. They more usually attend a gathering at which only ladies are present.

Ideally, Arab food should be provided, but the international cuisine produced by most of the first-class hotels is fast becoming acceptable, and even the norm. Because the Arabs are so hospitable and spare no expense or effort to entertain their guests, a foreigner should, within reason, do the same. In addition to the obvious requirement for good food in pleasant surroundings you could also consider other ideas that will make the occasion enjoyable e.g. a corner of the reception room could be set aside for an exhibition of paintings, a short film shown or a local musical group could play at the entrance to the reception. At a business function the guests are sometimes given a small memento on departure.

FESTIVALS

A number of religious festivals *(Eids)* are celebrated each year in the Muslim calendar (Details of Muslim festivals are given in Chapter 1). The foreigner really need only pay special attention to two of them, the *Eid Al-Adha* and the *Eid Al-Fitr*.

Eid Al-Adha
Eid Al-Fitr

3

The *Eid Al-Adha* comes at the end of the Hajj pilgrimage and the Eid Al-Fitr at the end of the month-long fast of Ramadan. As explained in Chapter 1 under *The Five Pillars of Islam – Fasting*, during this fast, all Muslims (with some exceptions such as travellers, the sick and small children) are required to abstain from food, drink, tobacco and all other pleasurable pursuits between sunrise and sunset. This can be a great burden especially if the month of fasting falls in summer. Naturally foreigners should be considerate in Ramadan and during daylight hours refrain from smoking, eating or drinking in the presence of Muslims or in public places. In any case, in most countries of the region it is a punishable offence to do so. It is also incumbent on foreign women to dress respectably during Ramadan.

Eid Cards

Greeting
cards

On the occasion of both the *Eids* it is customary to send cards of congratulation to your Arab friends and colleagues and if you are an official or a businessman, to those people with whom you frequently deal. The cards contain an appropriate greeting and message of congratulation in Arabic, some being suitable for both Eids and others being specific to a particular Eid. These cards can either be bought locally or at an international Arabic bookseller. Some large institutions and companies often have their own cards specially printed which include their logo and perhaps the name of the executive who will sign it, printed in Arabic. (*See* Chapter 6 – *Translations into Arabic*, pp 138-9.) It is the custom to sign the card and it should be dispatched to arrive a day to two in advance of the Eid. The approximate dates of Eids are given in Chapter 1 – *The Muslim Calendar.*

The recipient of an *Eid* card will occasionally return the compliment by sending a card of thanks, also signed. You could use the same type of card to thank an Arab for his card at Christmas. It is becoming an accepted custom to send 'Season's Greetings' cards at Christmas but this is normally done by a Muslim to a Christian and not the other way round.

Verbal *Eid* Congratulations

When meeting an Arab on the day of an *Eid* or in the days closely following it, it is customary to shake hands and offer the following congratulatory greeting:

Greeting   *Eid mubaarak!* (congratulations on the *Eid*!)
Reply   *Allah yubaarak feek* (and to you)

3

Eid Calls

In addition, at the time of the *Eid*, it is customary for prominent citizens to receive callers in their homes and palaces. A foreigner living in or visiting the region at this time should certainly consider calling on an Arab he knows well. Take local advice on the most appropriate time to call. The visit is brief unless you are asked to stay on for a meal. You enter the reception room, congratulate your host on the *Eid* as advised above and take a seat. Provided that it does not detract too much from the ceremony being conducted by the host, you may also congratulate others present – senior members of your host's family or someone you know. There then follows some general social conversation, coffee is served and after a short pause you should depart saying goodbye to your host and whoever else seems appropriate.

Arab families also visit each other at *Eid* time. If you know an Arab family well you would be welcome to call, perhaps taking a small gift for the children but, again, seek local advice on what is considered appropriate in a particular circumstance. Finally, it is customary to give your servants a reasonable gift of money at the time of each Eid. (*See* Chapter 5 – *Servants.*)

MISCELLANEOUS CUSTOMS

Admiration

Exercise care in admiring anything belonging to an Arab. If you do so too effusively, it is traditional for him to be honour bound to offer it to you as a gift, and even if you succeed in refusing it, it will take a long time!

3

Gifts

An Arab may not proffer thanks for a formal gift. This is a traditional custom, although it is changing and is coming more into line with the international practice of expressing thanks. An Arab may politely refuse a gift, indicating that you should not have taken the trouble. This refusal may be repeated but it is correct to insist on acceptance.

Thank you

Sometimes when an Arab says 'Thank you' he means 'No', for example when replying to an offer of refreshment, etc. This works in much the same way as *merci* used in French. If you wish to accept when something is offered simply say 'Yes'.

Animals

Whereas Arabs love horses, and hawks, and have a great respect for the camel, dogs are generally considered unclean and will not be approached or touched (except perhaps for the Saluki – the Arabian gazelle hound).

Congratulations

Congratulations should be offered to an Arab on the occasion of any achievement such as a promotion and it always gives a good impression to say this in Arabic:

Greeting   *Mabrook!* (Congratulations!)
Reply   *Allah yubaarak feek* (God bless you)

Public Prayers

It is not done to take undue notice of or interfere with someone who is praying in a public place such as an airport lounge, or in the market place (*souq*). It is also best to avoid walking in front of someone while they are praying.

Beckoning

One should never beckon anyone by using the forefinger of the right hand. This gesture has an offensive connotation in the Arab world (as it generally does in Mediterranean countries). It is better not to beckon at all, but if you do, then put all the fingers of the right hand downwards and pull the hand towards the body saying *'ta'aal'* (come).

ARAB NAMES

The first thing to do when writing to an Arab or meeting him is to get his name right. Arab names can be complicated to spell and may be transliterated from Arabic into English in a number of ways. The best solution is to use the version written by the Arab himself, e.g. on his card or letter heading. Note that two names may sound the same but there may be slight, but important differences: Mo**ham**med is different from Mah**mood**, **Maa**jid different from Maj**eed**, and Sal**eem** different from **Saa**lim. In addition, Mohammed is sometimes shortened to Mohd., and the apostrophe is used to represent a glottal stop, e.g. Sa'aad.

Arab names usually consist of three names – the indi-vidual's name followed by that of their father and grandfather or possibly the family name. The names are sometimes linked by *bin* or *ibn* meaning 'son of' or, in the case of a woman, by *bint*, meaning 'daughter of' or 'girl'. For example, a man's full name might be Ali Mo**ham**med **Has**san or Ali bin Mo**ham**med bin Hassan. He would probably not use all of the names being commonly known as Ali Mohammed. His sister in the same way would be called **Faa**tima bint Mo**ham**med bint **Has**san. Many Arab women do not use their husband's name but in certain circumstances, for example if an Arab is living in a Western country, a married woman may use her husband's last name and call herself, for example, Mrs **Has**san. If you need to know a woman's name, it is best to enquire what form she uses.

Certain Arab names are compounded with a prefix or a suffix:

* *Abdul* in front of a name, meaning literally the 'servant of', which is followed by an attribute to God,

Arab names

3

such as Abdul-Rah**maan** meaning 'servant of the merciful'. Aways refer to him by his full name, Abdul-Rah**maan**, and never simply 'Abdul'.

◆ *Abu* meaning 'father of'. A man may be known as Abu Mohammed, – 'the father of Mohammed'. It is only applied to the first born son and would be used particularly for the first few days after the birth. *Abu* is sometimes used figuratively, e.g. Abu Shanab meaning 'father of the moustache'. Sometimes a nickname such as Abu Nimr (father of the lion) takes the place of the real name.

◆ *Umm* meaning 'mother of' is used by a woman as part of, or in place of, her real name; e.g. Umm Kalthoom, the mother of Kalthoom, was a famous Egyptian singer.

◆ *Al* or *El* in front of the family name, often hyphenated. It is generally used to indicate a royal or distinguished family, e.g. Al-Nahyan, the ruling family of Abu Dhabi.

◆ The suffix *Ad-Din* (pronounced Ad-Deen), also written *Eddin*, means 'of the faith', e.g. Salah Ad-Din (Saladin) meaning 'the rightness of the faith'.

The above explains why, when you visit the region, the immigration forms ask you for your own name, your father's name and your family name.

FORMS OF ADDRESS AND OFFICIAL CORRESPONDENCE

You should address an Arab in speech or in writing by using his first name with the appropriate prefix, if there is one, for example, 'How do you do, Shaikh Mohammed?' In writing, foreign correspondents tend increasingly to follow the Western practice of addressing 'Dear Mr Mohammed', or 'Dear Mohammed', if you know him well. When an Arab travels abroad he would usually conform to Western practice by booking himself into an hotel as Mr Al-Kitbi or Mr A. Al-Kitbi.

Foreigners in the Arab world are referred to in the same way as an Arab would be, thus Mr James Peters would find himself addressed as Mr James rather than Mr Peters.

If you wish to call to someone or attract their attention it is not considered polite to call their name baldly. In this circumstance all names, titles and ranks are prefixed by *Ya* which can be literally translated as 'Oh'! Therefore if you called Ahmed you would say *Ya Ahmed*. This is used even in intimate speech to a friend, who would for example be addressed as *Ya Akhi*! ('Oh brother!').

Forms of address are generally more formal in the Arab world than in the West, with greater deference and respect being shown to those in authority or to senior members of the family. A guide to the various forms of address is given below.

Titles

Title	*English*	*Arabic*
Ambassador	Your Excellency	*Ya Sa'aadat As-Safeer* (initially) *Sa'aadatak* (thereafter)
Amir (Kuwait & Qatar)	Your Highness	*Ya Samoo Al-Ameer*
Crown Prince	Your Highness	*Ya Saahib As-Samoo*
Deputy (i.e. MP)	Your Excellency	*Ya Sa'aadat An-Na'ib* (initially) *Sa'aadatak* (thereafter)
Director or manager of a firm	Mr (Abdulla Fahid)	*Ya Sa'aadat Al-Mūdeer* (initially) *Sa'aadatak* or *Ya Mūdeer* (thereafter)
Doctor	Dr Ahmed	*Ya Doktoor Ahmed*
Engineer	Engineer Ahmed	*Ya Mūhandis*
Imaam	Your Eminence	*Ya Fadeelat Al-Imaam*
King (Bahrain)	Your Majesty[1]	*Ya Jalaalat Al-Malik* (initially) *Ya Jalaalatkūm* (thereafter)

Note 1. The King of Saudi Arabia is an exception. *See* Country Annex.

3 Titles

Title	English	Arabic
Minister (of government)	Your Excellency	*Ya Ma'aalee Al-Wozeer* (initially) Sir (thereafter)
Mohammed (familiar)	*Ya Mohammed*	*Ya Mohammed*
Mr Mohammed (formal)	Mr *Mohammed*	*Ya Seiyyid Mohammed* or *Ya Seiyyid*
President (of a State)	Mr President	*Ya Fakhaamat Ar-Ra'ees*
President (of a company or organisation)	Mr President	*Ya Sa'aadat Ar-Ra'ees*
Prime Minister	Prime Minister	*Ya Dowlat Ar-Ra'ees*
Prince (Royal)[1]	Your Royal Highness	*Ya Sahib As-Samoo Al-Maliki*
Princes (Other)	Your Highness	*Ya Saahib As-Samoo*
Private citizen	Mr Mohammed Hassan	*Ya Seiyyid*
Professor or learned person	Professor	*Ya Ūstadh* (also *Ūstaz*) (initially) *Seedee* (thereafter)
Ruling Shaikh (and some immediate family)	Your Highness	*Ya Samoo As-Sheikh*
Shaikh (others of ruling family)	Shaikh . . . (name)	*Ya Samoo As-Sheikh*
Shaikh (not hereditary)[2]	Shaikh . . . (name)	*Ya Sheikh... (name)*
Stranger	No equivalent	*Hadritak* or *Seeyaadatak*
Sultan of Oman	Your Majesty	*Ya Jalaalat As-Sultaan*
Waiter or servant	Waiter	*Ya Akhi* (lit: Oh Brother)
Woman	Mrs Hassan	*Ya Saiyyida* or *Ya Sit*

Note 1. In Saudi Arabia sons and grandsons of King Abdul Aziz ibn Saud are addressed as 'Your Royal Highness'.
Note 2. *Shaikh* or *Sheikh.* Besides being a hereditary title used by

members of the ruling families of the Arab Gulf states it is also given to the leaders of tribes, senior members of leading families, religious leaders, and judges. Also to those who have achieved distinction in the community, usually in later life, as a mark of popular respect. It has also the literal meaning in Arabic of 'an old and revered person'.

Military and Police Ranks

For reference purposes, the most common Arabic words used for military and police ranks are:

Military titles

Fareeq Awwal – General
Fareeq – Lieutenant-General
Liwa – Major-General
Ameed – Brigadier
Aqeed – Colonel
Mūqoddam – Lieutenant-Colonel
Raa'id – Major
Naqeeb – Captain
Mūlaazim Awal – Lieutenant

*Mūlaazim **Thaanee*** – Second-Lieutenant
*Wokeel Awwa*l – Warrant Officer Class I
Wokeel – Warrant Officer Class 2
Raqeeb Awwal – Staff Sergeant
Raqeeb Sergeant
Areef – Corporal
Wokeel Areef – Lance-Corporal
*Jūn*dee – Private

Official Correspondence

A letter to an Arab may be written in English. In some circumstances (particularly in Saudi Arabia) it is best to write both in Arabic and English. The form it takes depends upon the exact situation and it is advisable to seek expert advice on this important topic. Be sure that your adviser is fully conversant with local usage, as terms and form can differ from country to country. (Guidance on translation services is given in Chapter 6.) As an example, a formal letter to a senior figure would open:

Letters

> Your Excellency,
> After greetings
> I am honoured to inform you etc

and end, if a business letter, with for example:

> Finally, Your Excellency, please be assured of our best attention at all times.

CHAPTER FOUR

Visiting the Peninsula

INTRODUCTION

The purpose of this chapter is to provide essential advice and a check-list for the planning and conduct of a visit to the region. Points applicable only to business travellers are included in Chapter 6.

TIMING A VISIT

Climate
The climatic conditions vary between countries and even within a country, depending on the height above sea level and distance from the coast. The best time to visit is in the spring or autumn, but high summer temperatures are not necessarily uncomfortable, particularly if the atmosphere is dry – as it is for example in Riyadh. But if the heat is accompanied by high humidity, as in most coastal areas, the combination can be unpleasant. Heat and humidity may both be largely irrelevant, however, if you intend to spend most of the time in air-conditioned hotels, offices and cars – which are now the norm throughout the region. Details of climate are included in the Country Annexes at the back of the book.

Heat and humidity

The Calendar
As well as the time of year and the climate, consider the Muslim calendar and the effect of visiting during Ramadan when the normal routine of life can be disrupted, the major festivals and the annual summer holidays from the end of July to the beginning of September. A visit at festival time can, however, be an interesting experience. The approximate forecast dates of the major religious festivals are given in Chapter 1, and national holidays in the Country Annexes.

Ramadan

CLOTHING

It would be wrong to imagine that it is always very hot in the region. In winter it is often cold, windy and wet and at such times European clothing is entirely appropriate. It

4

Dressing for
the occasion

is best to double check just before your visit. In the summer months, a range of lightweight clothing is necessary, preferably made of cotton, since other materials such as man-made fibres can irritate the skin. Appropriate items include lightweight suits and cotton shirts, underclothes and socks. It is particularly important that shoes are loose-fitting and made of leather since feet swell appreciably in the heat, and need to breathe.

For men, the appropriate dress for official visits to an Arab in his office or when attending a formal function is a suit and tie. For less formal occasions, an open neck shirt and slacks are suitable. For casual wear sandals or desert boots (fawn coloured suede with rubber composition soles) are popular and can be purchased locally. Good walking shoes or boots may also be useful. Even in summer the evenings can be quite cold and you may need light wollen jumpers, or a shawl for a woman.

For women, cotton dresses or skirts and tops are probably the most suitable summer wear, but these should conform with the advice given on *Standards of Dress* below.

Hats have long ceased to be an article of formal attire but anyone who intends to spend time in the open should protect themselves from the sun, particularly in summer. They can easily be bought locally. Sunglasses are advisable for every visitor.

It is possible to get clothes tailor-made at reasonable prices in the region. It is common practice to ask a local tailor to copy an existing suit or dress, and this they often do very well. Long term visitors in particular should seek first-hand advice in this regard when putting their wardrobes together. Beautiful kaftans and shawls can also be bought in the bazaars.

Standards of Dress

Foreign visitors should always be sensitive to local sensibilities in this regard. Custom varies considerably within the region. In Saudi Arabia, for example, women are required to cover their arms and legs in public (*See* General Comments in Saudi Arabia Annex), while in other countries of the Peninsula modest Western dress would be the norm.

As a general rule, male visitors should wear long trousers (shorts are not approved of) and a shirt with a collar in public places, and women should wear a modestly cut dress with sleeves and a skirt covering her knees. Whatever the country, Arab men and women are genuinely offended when they see foreigners dressed in scanty and pro-vocatively cut clothing in such public places as the bazaar. For the same reason it is not acceptable for a man to strip to the waist. Finally, one should not wear swimming costumes away from the immediate vicinity of the beach or pool.

Anyone visiting the region on business will find that the Arabs they meet are always immaculately attired in the traditional long flowing robe or Western-style suits and they naturally expect foreigners who claim their attention to be equally well dressed. Appearances count for a lot.

Finally, for foreigners to wear the traditional Arab dress is not regarded with favour, as it is fast becoming the dress which distinguishes a national citizen. It would cause offence, and in Oman it is against the law. For similar reasons the foreigner should not carry prayer beads unless he is a Muslim.

HEALTH

Vaccinations and Immunisation
Before you travel check if any vaccinations are necessary, following the advice of the relevant embassy in the UK and the FCO Travel Advice (website: www.fco.gov.uk). Vaccinations must always be spaced out, so you should consult a doctor or vaccination clinic at least two months prior to departure, particularly if children are involved.

Malaria
There is a risk of infection in some parts of the region. Your GP can obtain advice on the prophylactic appropriate to each area from the Malarial Reference Laboratory at the London School of Hygiene and Tropical Medicine. Anti-malarial tablets are taken prior to, during, and after a visit, as prescribed by a doctor, so check well in advance of your visit.

4

BEWARE OF THE HEAT!

SUNBURN

Even mild sunburn can be uncomfortable. To avoid being burnt, start by exposing the body for a short period each day; ten minutes is enough on the first day. Use protective lotions and avoid the heat of the day from about 11 a.m. to 3 p.m., even on cloudy days when the sun's rays still penetrate.

PRICKLY HEAT

Increased exposure to sunlight combined with perspiration and tightly fitting clothes can cause a red itching rash known as prickly heat, which is cured by showering regularly, drying thoroughly and applying powder.

HEAT EXHAUSTION AND HEAT STROKE

In the summer heat it is important to consume adquate amounts of water and salt. A person working in the open needs up to 12 pints a day. Add enough salt to your food so that you can taste it, and always drink water with your meal. Salt tablets are not recommended. Dehydration, producing listlessness, headaches, dizziness, nausea and a high temperature are indicative of heat exhaustion. In extreme cases, a person will pass out, run a high temperature and stop perspiring. This condition is extremely serious and is termed heat stroke, and can cause permanent damage if untreated for long. For heat exhaustion and heat stroke the immediate treatment is to reduce the body temperature by any means possible, concentrating particularly on the head. One way is to apply a cold wet towel or ice and ensure that the patient is in a cool shady place. The next step is to increase the body's salt and water content by administering a saline drink. In the case of heat stroke, however, professional medical assistance should be always be sought as soon as possible. (The risk of dehydration is increased by drinking alcohol.)

Keep exposed parts of the body covered out of doors after sunset and use an insect repellent ointment or spray. Unless you are sleeping in air-conditioning, close the windows of your bedroom before sunset and spray the room with insecticide spray. For added protection, sleep under a mosquito net or burn a mosquito coil or tablet – a vapour-emitting impregnated substance heated by an electrical element, although the vapour emitted can be a little strong for some. A new version of this electrical device is now available, and uses an odourless clear liquid in place of the traditional tablets. All of these can be bought locally.

4

Insect
repellants

Travellers under Medication

Pharmacies in the region are invariably well stocked. However, travellers under special medication may be advised to take essential supplies with them with a spare, signed prescription as an additional precaution. Medicines should be clearly labelled with their pharmaceutical name and it is prudent in these days of sensitivity to the carriage of drugs, particularly in Saudi Arabia, to carry a certificate from a doctor explaining the situation. Restrictions exist on the importation of a range of drugs into Saudi Arabia, including tranquillisers and sleeping pills. For advice in the UK, call the Home Office Drugs Branch on telephone +44 (0)20 7273 3806. Finally, the trade names of some drugs differ from country to country, so it worth checking before you travel if you are likely to need a specific branded medicine.

Medical Insurance

It is essential to take out full medical insurance when visiting the region. Although medical facilities (doctors, hospitals, clinics and pharmacies) are extremely good in all countries except the Republic of Yemen, there is no reciprocal health-care agreement between the countries of the Peninsula and the UK, and visitors will have to pay for treatment, which can be costly. Insurance should be comprehensive and include repatriation to your home country in case of need. Check whether your insurance

4

cover stipulates that you pay when receiving treatment and reclaim the cost later, or whether payment is made by the insurance company direct to a hospital or doctor.

Medical Emergencies

As has been mentioned, the medical facilities in the region – doctors, dentists, hospitals and the ancilliary services – are of a generally high standard. In the event of an emergency you can seek treatment at any clinic or hospital. However, these facilities are not always free for foreigners and you should indicate your willingness to pay a fee and carry evidence of any medical insurance to ensure you receive prompt treatment.

Health insurance

ENTRY REQUIREMENTS

Visas

All countries in the region require the visitor to have a valid passport which for some countries must extend for six months after the intended visit. Most countries object to evidence of a visit to Israel. Visas are obtained from relevant embassies and consulates by applying in person, by post, through your travel agent and, for some countries, can be obtained on arrival. Details of the current requirements for each country are given in the Country Annexes.

A visa application form is usually presented with a passport, one or two photographs and a small fee. Visa requirements, particularly health regulations, change from time to time and the responsible embassy or travel agent will update you. If you attend the embassy in person you will be given a receipt for your passport, or a paper with a reference number on it, and you will be asked to call back later for your visa – anything between two days and two weeks, depending on the time of year.

Passports

When you get your visa make sure you understand the exact extent of its validity. If you are landing or transiting through a third country on the way to your main destination, a transit visa may also be required.

Single parents or adults travelling with children

should be aware that some countries require documentary evidence of parental responsibility before allowing them to enter the country, and, in some cases, before permitting the children to leave. It is advisable to clarify this point when applying for your visa.

4

CURRENCY

Except in the Republic of Yemen (*see* Country Annex) travellers' cheques, major Western currencies and credit cards (e.g. Visa and Mastercard) are readily accepted and most British debit cards can be used to obtain funds from banks and ATM outlets. As elsewhere in the world, the exchange rate in a Bureau de Change is likely to be better than an hotel cashier. Always check carefully the figures on of notes and coins to avoid expensive mistakes. The Arabic for 50, for example, is very similar to 500 and unfortunately the larger denomination notes are often smaller than those of lesser value, as is true of some coinage. Arabic numerals are illustrated in Chapter 2.

Cash and credit cards

There are restrictions on the amounts of currency that can be taken into some countries of the region and it is wise to check this at the time you apply for your visa. Be careful not to break any currency rules as such offences are taken very seriously.

PROHIBITED GOODS

There are restrictions on a number of imports to the region, with each country having its own rules. The main prohibitions are covered below and details are included in the Country Annexes, but the latest regulations should be checked with the relevant embassy or travel agent.

Banned imports

Drugs
Drugs offences are viewed as extremely serious crimes throughout the region, and in Saudi Arabia, Oman, UAE and Kuwait can carry the death penalty (*see* Country Annexes). Care should be taken to ensure that prescribed

97

4

medications are not confused with illicit drugs (*see Travellers under Medication* above).

Alcohol
Alcohol is strictly forbidden in Saudi Arabia, Kuwait and Sharjah (UAE). In Bahrain, Oman and the UAE, visitors are permitted to bring in a small quantity of duty free alcohol (Oman by air only). In these countries and in Qatar, alcohol is available in some hotels, and non-Muslims and expatriates are allowed a quota for personal consumption on being granted a special license. Penalties for alcohol-related offences are severe in all countries, particularly in Saudi Arabia. *See* Chapter 5 – *Local Laws and Customs*, and the country annexes.

Food
Import of pork is also forbidden on religious grounds.

Publications and Videos
Avoid carrying any literature of a politically controversial nature, or non-Islamic religious material, which may be confiscated. Care must be taken over what is considered in the region as pornographic literature. Adult magazines of the *Playboy* type fall into this category. Any publication with nude pictures may offend a Muslim's religious sensibilities. Western publications on sale in the region and in particular in Saudi Arabia are censored. Videos are regarded with suspicion by the customs authorities and may be confiscated. In Saudi Arabia the authorities will insist on viewing them before allowing them to be imported. It is most unwise to attempt to conceal them on arrival.

ARRIVAL

Immigration Forms
Because of the way Arab names are written, an immigration form will ask for your own, your father's and your family name. You should simply equate this to your first name, any second name and your surname. The form will also ask for your address in the country and your sponsor. Put your hotel

or if you have no pre-arranged accommodation, your Embassy and your sponsor/agent's address.

Customs Formalities

It is not unusual for the customs officials in a Peninsula country to carry out a search of your baggage on arrival and in Saudi Arabia it is always done. The official will first request your passport and then ask you to open each item of luggage, which he will systematically search. You should appreciate that the official is required to ensure that no drugs or prohibited items are imported into the Kingdom. He is aware that the majority of foreigners are unlikely to transgress the local laws and if you are polite and cooperative, the search will often only be a cursory one.

Transportation

If possible, arrange to be met and taken direct to your accommodation. Anything that cuts down the hassle and time taken in battling out of an airport is a good thing. However, buses, taxis and self-drive cars are available at all the region's airports. Taxis are generally cheap but it is best either to go by the meter or to agree the price before the start of a journey to avoid any argument later over the fare.

Car hire and taxis

Although cars can be conveniently hired and insurance cover is adequate, an accident does result in delays and other complications (*see Emergencies and Car Accidents* below). It is, for example, obligatory to stay at the scene of an accident until the police arrive in order to establish blame – which may take some time. For this reason, on a short visit it may be better to use taxis or hire a car with a driver.

If you wish to hire a self-drive car, you will need a Western driving licence and possibly an International Driving Licence/Permit as well. The regulations differ from country to country and it is best to check beforehand with the hire company, your travel agent or the relevant embassy. In UK, an International Licence can be obtained from the AA or RAC (members only) and most Post Offices, on production of a current UK licence two passport photographs, a photocopy of your passport ID

Driving licences

and a small fee. Ensure you fully understand the local traffic procedures and laws and what action must be taken by the driver in the event of an accident. Check the extent of cover provided by the insurance in respect of the vehicle, passengers and third parties. Also check the extent to which an accident might delay your return home.

Security

Arabs are generally extremely law-abiding and the Arab countries traditionally safe places to visit. However, the current threat of terrorism, including attacks on Westerners, means that all visitors to the region must give serious attention to the question of personal security. UK nationals are strongly advised to follow the advice of the Foreign and Comonwealth Office (FCO) given in the Travel Advice section of their website (www.fco.gov.uk) or by telephoning their Travel Advice Unit on 0870 606 0209. The FCO website also has contact details for the US State Department and some other allied governments, as well as important information on local laws.

Although the incidence of other types of crime is generally low, thefts do occur. It is best to lock valuables in a safe place and avoid either carrying a large sum of money or leaving it lying around in a hotel room or on a beach. Keep a photocopy of the main pages of your passport and any important personal documents. Carry your passport or some other means of identification with you in a secure place during any excursion outside your hotel.

Photography

Although cameras and camcorders are permitted in places of architectural interest, elsewhere they must be used with care. It is forbidden to photograph military installations or airfields, ports and even bridges. Some people also object to being photographed, and you should ask permission first. You should always avoid photographing women. A Polaroid camera can be a novel way of getting on with people you meet on desert trips in remote areas, but you should always explain or illustrate the device before photographing them.

Visiting Mosques

In a few Arab countries foreign visitors are permitted to enter mosques. However, it is obligatory to be soberly dressed, to remove your shoes (slippers may be provided) and for women to wear a head scarf.

Bargaining in the Market (*Sooq*)

Bargaining is in the Arab blood. It has been described as the art of compromise without backing down or losing face. Many foreigners either find bargaining tedious or else are ignorant of how to go about it, but in the Peninsula it is a way of life. Some shops, especially if they sell basic commodities, have fixed prices but market stalls do not and the seller and the buyer will haggle to get the best price possible. Sellers are often surprised – and, one suspects, a little disappointed – when a foreigner pays the asking price without a quibble.

4

BARGAINING POWER

To bargain you need time. You will compare the asking price with the going rate for an article. If you don't know it, then decide what you are willing to pay. Then convince the seller that you are quite prepared to do without the item and are willing to walk away. If you show that you are at all keen, the seller will hold out for a high price – and get it! If the shopkeeper quotes a price of 10 Dinars for example but you decide it is worth 7, then offer him 5. He may come down to 8 and you can then rise to 6, letting him push you to 7. If you stick out for a low price do nevertheless leave him some room for manoeuvre or he will not be able to meet your offer without losing face. Perhaps the most important aspect of any negotiation is to remain on good terms at all times. The haggling may become heated, but if it becomes personal, or the shopkeeper decides he does not like you, he may well decide not to deal with you, even if it is to his detriment. Personal relationships are again all-important and you should not be surprised if a shopkeeper offers you tea and is not at all offended if you leave without buying.

General Emergencies and Car Accidents

Car accidents

If you are involved in an incident such as an infringement of the law or a car accident, the cardinal rule is to remain calm, polite and at all costs avoid a confrontation, however unpleasant the situation and however strong the provocation. Even minor expressions of road rage, such as rude gestures, can be severely penalised. It may be difficult to make yourself understood to a local with little or no English but keep calm and use the basic Arabic emergency phrases given in Chapter 2.

In the event of a car accident, you are required by law in most Peninsula countries to remain on the scene until the traffic police arrive. However slight the damage, never move the vehicle. The police will make out an accident report which will usually apportion blame and will give you a copy which it is necessary before the car can legally be repaired. If someone is killed or injured, the police usually arrest or detain the driver and possibly the passengers, until blame is established and legal

Drunkenness

proceedings are completed. For this reason it is vital not only to carry your passport at all times but also a list of emergency telephone numbers, such as your embassy consul, sponsor or hotel.

The law in the Peninsula countries is particularly strict with regard to displays of drunkenness in public places and in the case of drink-driving the police will immediately imprison you until you come before a judge. This may take several days and punishments are severe – either a heavy fine or prison sentence and, in Saudi Arabia, possibly corporal punishment as well.

You may also appeal for assistance and advice to your local sponsor or the Consul at your embassy. An explanation of UK Foreign and Commonwealth Office Consular Services Abroad is summarised in the Annexes.

DEPARTURE

Many Arab countries impose an airport tax on departure, usually payable in the local currency. It is wise to keep back a small amount of local currency to pay this.

CHAPTER FIVE

The Expatriate

INTRODUCTION
ASSESSING AND PREPARING FOR A POST
EXPATRIATE LIFE
THE FEMALE EXPATRIATE
DESERT TRAVEL

INTRODUCTION

This chapter gives guidance on the essential considerations for those contemplating taking up residence in the Peninsula. It outlines the main types of expatriate employment, how to assess and prepare for the post, and some of the major facets of expatriate life.

Many thousands of expatriates are employed in the Gulf countries and Saudi Arabia, the result of rapid development and a shortage of qualified labour, among other factors. Broadly speaking, it is mainly Europeans and North Americans who fill the managerial and specialist posts while those from the Far East, the Indian sub-continent, Africa and other Arab countries work mainly in the service industries. The majority of expatriates are male but there is a significant number of females working as nurses, teachers, house servants etc. Understandably, the policy in all the Peninsula countries is to reduce their reliance on foreign labour and increase employment for Nationals, an aim which is being slowly but steadily achieved.

Expatriate life can be an enjoyable and rewarding experience, particularly when shared with one's family. For those employed by a Western-based organisation or large Arab institution such as a national government or oil company, expatriate employment means tax-free pay, generous benefits and a higher than usual standard of living. Housing, home leave and other benefits are typically provided free of charge or there will be allowances in lieu. Most Western expatriates have a house servant and lead an active social life, and there is generally ample scope for leisure and sporting activities.

The expatriate working for a private Arab company, perhaps as a professional advisor or employee, may find that although the contract, terms and conditions and lifestyle will usually be similar to other categories of expatriate, his employment may be less secure and success will depend very much on the personal relationship with the Arab employer.

5

Nationaliities

5

Finally, it is worth emphasising that while the Peninsula countries have much in common, living conditions, and therefore expatriate life, differ significantly from country to country and within countries themselves. Life in Dubai, for example, which caters for Western tastes in a number of ways, contrasts markedly with Saudi Arabia, where alcohol is forbidden and the way of life is much more conservative. Even within Saudi Arabia itself conditions differ, and expatriates will find life in Jeddah more relaxed than in Riyadh. The general characteristics of each Peninsula country are described in the Country Annexes but advice is given in this chapter on researching the detailed, up-to-date, situation in each country.

CULTURE SHOCK

Culture shock is a perfectly natural phenomenon which affects us all when making a major move into an unfamiliar environment. It occurs to some degree or other when you move home in your own country, but the move to such a fundamentally different culture as the Arabian Peninsula, combined with the inevitable stress of reorganising your personal life, can be traumatic. If often affects wives more than husbands, since a husband's work takes his mind off other things. A husband needs to be particularly sympathetic in this regard. The reaction from culture shock is a negative one, varying from mild to serious, and everyone experiences it, even if they do not care to admit it. However, if it is not to spoil an otherwise enjoyable experience in one's life, it is important to take positive steps to combat it. Among the proven measures are: to be well briefed, to understand and rationalise the cultural differences, and to make sure that you are well equipped for your hobbies, sporting and leisure activities. Perhaps the single most important step to take, particularly for a wife, is to talk to someone who lives, or has lived, in the country you are going to. Personal advice from a sensible, experienced expatriate is invaluable.

ASSESSING AND PREPARING FOR A POST

Everyone going to the region for the first time experiences something of a culture shock and some find that they are not suited to expatriate life. The successful expatriate needs to be adaptable, with a measure of self-reliance and also a sensitivity to life in a completely different culture. A study of the preceding chapters will help to explain what is entailed in this regard. It must be said that anyone with a short temper, which is bound to be exacerbated by the hot climate and the inevitable frustrations, will almost certainly fail.

Adapting to the life

The cost of failure can be surprisingly high; not only will it adversely affect the company's business but an individual's career and well-being, not to mention that of his family. When it happens that a person is clearly wrong for a particular job, it often transpires with the value of hindsight, that the individual or the recruiter failed to make an accurate assessment beforehand.

It costs a Western company in the region of £100,000 a year to appoint and maintain a senior manager in the Peninsula and so it is worth making as thorough an appraisal as possible.

The main points for consideration in assessing an expatriate post are outlined below.

Briefing

Most Western expatriates in the Peninsula are recruited by a commercial company or recruitment agency with experience of the region. They should provide the expatriate with an adequate job specification, the terms and conditions of employment, and information on the expatriate lifestyle, the bad points as well as the good. It is vital to be well informed and if possible you should obtain the views of at least one independent source with recent experience.

Preparation courses

Ideally, an expatriate, along with his spouse and any teenage children should attend a course of preparation such as those run at the Farnham Castle International Briefing and Conference Centre in Surrey. Scheduled courses for countries in the Middle East are run at regular

5

intervals and cover the complete range of information required to achieve a speedy and effective transition to the new role for the assignee and his/her family. It also offers the opportunity to meet and network with other assignees moving to the same region, or very often the same country. Courses can be tailor-made, and give comprehensive information on the political, economic, social life and laws of the country they are going to and include talks by expatriates with recent experience. Contact details: The Client Services Team, Farnham Castle International Briefing and Conference Centre, Farnham Castle, Castle Street, Surrey GU9 OAG. Tel: 01252 720418; Fax: 01252 719277; Website www.farnhamcastle.com; E-mail: info@farnhamcastle.com.

Contract, Salary, Terms and Conditions.

If the post is accompanied, the minimum term of contract will usually be two years, and a minimum of one year if the post is bachelor status. It is important to get the terms of the contract correct at the outset, when one is in a stronger negotiating position, as it is difficult if not impossible to improve on it later on. Concentrate on the essential elements rather than niggling over details, although occasionally these can be important. It will be helpful, for instance, to ascertain how the contract compares with those of other expatriates of a similar status. Also consider what financial and other safeguards are included if, through no fault of your own, you do not complete the predicted period of your contract.

Financial safeguards

If considering a post working directly for a private Arab company you should acquaint yourself with local employment law and the safeguards it provides. A local lawyer will advise you. Your embassy can usually recommend one specialising in this field.

Judge the salary and benefits offered against the local cost of living. Double check the cost of living with someone who is living in, or has recent experience of, the country you are going to. You might be paid in the local currency which is either directly linked to or tends to follow the US dollar. You will therefore need to follow

Exchange rates

the value of the local currency against the dollar, in relation to local spending power and funds you intend to repatriate. Most Peninsula currencies do not fluctuate a great deal against each other or the US dollar, although it could be a significant consideration if your contract were to run for several years. It is as well to have a contingency arrangement in place from the outset.

Finally, consider your overall financial situation. The advice of an accountant well versed in finance for expatriates is vital. Consider carefully your qualification for UK tax-free status and the ramifications of returning to the UK before the end of the period stipulated by the Inland Revenue. Also consider the effect, if any, on pensions, UK property, investments (particularly offshore), overseas banking, National Insurance Contributions, payment of VAT and duty on overseas purchases such as cars. Recruiters often offer comprehensive information on all these aspects but it is still sensible to obtain independent advice. Yemen is the only Peninsula country to levy income tax at present.

Tax and investment

5

Benefits and Allowances

Multinationals usually provide their expatriates with furnished accommodation, electricity, water, housing maintenance, children's education, and sometimes transportation to work as well as a servant, although the latter may depend on the seniority of the appointment. Also provided may be family membership of a recreational club, which is often the only activity available to Western expatiates and can be expensive.

The benefits mentioned above will either be provided by the employer or an allowance up to an agreed ceiling will be paid in lieu.

Removals

Assuming that fully furnished accommodation is provided, removal will normally only amount to transporting personal effects. A weight and capacity allowance will be given for removal by air or sea. Packing and insurance should be included. A modest increase in the return allowance is usually given to cover some purchases made during the tour.

5

Travel to and from Post and Leave

A two-year accompanied contract will certainly include free air travel to and from the Peninsula at the beginning and end of a tour and for annual leave. Tickets will be provided for the expatriate, his wife and any children accompanying him. One or two return tickets per year will also be provided for children at boarding school in their home country to visit their parents. Single expatriates will receive the same free travel to and from the Peninsula country and for annual leave. Bachelor status (married unaccompanied) expatriates will usually be given more frequent leave, again with air travel paid for, to compensate for separation from their spouses. The class of air travel varies according to the seniority of appointment. Some employers allow their expatriates to take cash in lieu of tickets, but experience has shown that it is never a good idea to forgo one's leave entirely to save money. A break is essential.

Accommodation

Expatriates are usually provided with a fully furnished flat or villa or an allowance in lieu. In the Gulf countries and Saudi Arabia this can cost several thousand pounds a year and the rent is sometimes required to be paid a year in advance. Electricity is usually provided free, since running air-conditioning is an expensive but essential facility. Other living expenses however, such as home contents insurance and private telephone bills are met by the expatriate. Insurance is easily arranged locally.

Cars

Western companies usually provide cars on the same basis as at home. Local Arab organisations may also provide transportation, and certainly to and from work for bachelor status posts. As far as personal vehicles are concerned, most makes of car can be purchased in the region but it may not be possible to buy and run a right-hand drive vehicle. Four-wheel drive vehicles are popular – and for desert trips are essential . Visits to the desert are a favourite expatriate pastime in the spring and autumn. Car maintenance facilities are generally good and fuel, as one might expect, is extremely cheap.

It is necesssary to have a residence permit before being legally permitted to obtain a local driving licence or purchase a car, and most people hire one in the interim. A local licence is usually granted on production of an International Driving Licence and/or a national one. (*See also* Chapter 4 – *Transportation, General Emergencies and Car Accidents.*)

Driving licenses

Health Care

5

Most Western employment contracts include the provision of free local private medical and dental care and repatriation to the home country in the event of serious illness for expatriates and their dependants. The employer may well provide this through local or international medical insurance. Full medical and dental checks should be carried out prior to departure.

An expatriate arriving in the summertime should avoid strenuous exercise until fully acclimatised. This can take anything from a week to a month.

Children's Education

In countries where there is a sizeable British, American or International community there will be fee-paying English-language and other primary schools of a reasonable standard, but secondary schools are less common. An expatriate contract often includes the cost of local education at these schools. Expatriates with older children sometimes arrange boarding-school education in the home country, in which case the contract usually covers the cost of air fares for at least two school holidays for children to visit their parents.

Arrival in a Peninsula country

Most employers arrange for the reception of their expatriates, usually through the company's local sponsor or representative office, and place them in a hotel or in temporary accommodation until a suitable villa or flat is ready. Then it will be necessary to tackle the (usually

Documents to carry

5

lengthy) administrative formalities, such as organising legal residence etc. Take with you all personal documentation such as birth, marriage, health, driving licences and, depending on the appointment, original certificates of education qualifications (e.g. your degree), plus a copious quantity of passport-sized photographs for yourself and your family. Photographs are needed for most applications. Local documentation includes a residence permit or visa, driving licence, a permit to purchase alcohol (in some countries) and possibly an identity card.

EXPATRIATE LIFE

Western expatriates have traditionally been highly regarded in the Peninsula countries. Their professionalism, integrity and ability to get on with the nationals is widely recognised.

A Representative Appointment

If an expatriate has been appointed to represent a Western company or organisation in the Peninsula he or she will have the task of reporting the local situation in terms which the parent company can understand. The views of the homebased head office will, of course, be based on their own priorities and business culture. They will usually have limited understanding of the Arab concept of time, the difficulty of access to those in authority, the local decision making process, the influences at work in society or indeed, the Arab culture generally. This should not become a consuming issue. However, it is incumbent on the expatriate representative to do all he can to meet the aims of his head office, intelligently interpreting their requirements and adapting them to suit the local scene. He should report back in as much detail as necessary but must never be tempted to colour information to justify bad news or to enhance his position. Honesty is the best long-term policy even if it is not fully understood or appreciated. It helps if one enjoys a close relationship with one's boss and is confident of his or her full support.

Reporting to HQ

Medical and Dental Treatment

The expatriate should sign-on with a doctor and dentist immediately on arrival. Most medical and dental care is a mixture of private clinics and government hospitals and some foreign firms issue their expatriates with a medical identification card to ensure cover in an emergency. Notes on health care are included in Chapter 4.

Local Laws and Customs

Most expatriates happily abide by local laws and customs and lead an enjoyable and trouble-free existence. Nevertheless, particularly in the more conservative countries of the Peninsula, problems arise either because expatriates are ignorant of local laws or, less frequently, because they disregard them.

It is important to realise that expatriates have no special legal status in an Arab country. They are subject to the law like everyone else. Diplomatic immunity is only granted to officially accredited diplomats. If an expatriate breaks the law and is arrested, his own embassy or government may petition on his behalf but would have no power to demand their release. An explanation of UK Foreign and Commonwealth Office Consular Services Abroad is summarised in the Annexes.

Legal status

Most legal problems are connected with driving, drink and drugs.

On driving, follow the advice given in the previous chapter under *Transportation*. It is usually best to travel as a passenger for the first week after arrival in order to get used to the local driving conditions and traffic regulations.

The laws on the consumption, possession and manufacture of alcohol are strict in all the Peninsula countries. In Saudi Arabia the penalty for the possession and consumption of alcohol is imprisonment, possible corporal punishment (flogging) and deportation. Alcohol is also forbidden in Kuwait and Sharjah. In some Peninsula countries Westerners are allowed to purchase alcohol in major hotels and to buy a quota for personal consumption. However, the misuse of this privilege, such

Alcohol

as over-indulgence in public or the consumption of alcohol while driving will lead to immediate arrest, a fine and possibly imprisonment. Expatriates need to make themselves fully aware of the latest local rules and regulations on arrival in a country. An outline of the current laws is contained in the Country Annexes.

Drugs

The laws relating to drugs are the most draconian. In Saudi Arabia, Kuwait, Oman and the UAE some drug-related crimes are a capital offence. Every visitor to Saudi Arabia will see a warning to this effect on his immigration entry form. In the remaining Peninsula countries, it is regarded as a serious offence punishable by imprisonment and eventual deportation.

Security

Security

As mentioned in Chapter 4, although Arabs are generally law-abiding and the Arab countries traditionally safe places in which to live, the current threat of terrorism, including attacks on Westerners, means that expatriates must give serious attention to the question of personal security. UK nationals are strongly advised to follow the advice of the Foreign and Commonwealth Office (FCO) given in the Travel Advice section of their website (www.fco.gov.uk). The website also has contact details for th US State Department and some other allied govern-ments and includes important information on local laws. Expatriates should register with their local consular office and follow any in-country advice issued by their embassy. In some countries there is a local warden scheme, and some multi-national companies institute their own security schemes for the added protection of their employees.

Working Hours and Recreation

Leisure time

The working week is from Saturday to Thursday lunch time although Thursday is increasingly becoming regarded as a holiday. In most Arab countries the working day starts early in the morning, finishes at 1 or 2 pm, and, after lunch and a siesta through the hottest part of the day, resumes in the late afternoon until around 6 or 7 pm. This leaves plenty of time for sport –

tennis, swimming, sailing or water-skiing. In Peninsula countries there are social and sporting clubs with facilities for all these activities. Sometimes the membership is restricted to Westerners in order to protect the culture and values of the local Muslim community. Friday, the holy day of the week, is universally treated as a holiday. In some countries the offices of foreign institutions such as Western embassies, are increasingly choosing to work on Thursday but take a two-day weekend on Friday and Saturday, which has the advantage of bringing their working week more into line with the head office in their home country.

Weekends

5

Domestic Servants

Many expatriates have a domestic servant of some sort, a nanny, cook or someone to help with housework. The servants are expatriates themselves, coming mostly from Africa and Asia. Servants are not as much of a luxury as they may sound and many people consider the climate is debilitating enough to make them a necessity.

Domestic Servants

You may take on a good servant from your predecessor or a friend, but otherwise you will have to recruit one. You should check the local employment laws with regard to employee rights, repatriation to their home country etc. An insurance policy of some sort is usually necessary to cover accidents in the home. Employ a new servant on a strictly probationary arrangement at the outset, e.g. on a month's trial.

Make sure you establish and maintain a correct relationship. Over-familiarity leads to a lack of respect and encourages a servant to lower standards and often to take advantage of their employer. The best sort of relationship is one of semi-informality – courteous and considerate but correct and always keeping one's distance.

Employer/ employee relationships

Because some servants are Muslims and their religious beliefs must be respected, do not ask a cook to prepare pork unless you are sure he is happy to do so. Make every allowance during the month-long fast of Ramadan when they will be short of sleep, hungry during the day and not able to work as hard or as long hours as usual. Servants, in common with all Muslims, have a holiday over the period of the *Eid Al-Adha* and the *Eid Al-Fitr* and should be given a reasonably generous gift of money for each *Eid*.

Making allowances

Never in their presence lose your temper or your dignity. Once you have shown a lack of control and probably wounded his pride as well, it will be difficult to re-establish an effective working relationship. There is one other danger which old hands will readily acknowledge. Think twice before blaming a servant if something goes missing or gets broken – remember that an accusation is impossible to retract and harder to redress if it proves unjustified.

Finally, sacking an incompetent or dishonest servant can be a tricky business. It is best to talk it over with an experienced colleague to minimise any personal animosity, safeguard your possessions and comply with local regulations. It is always preferable to pay money in lieu of notice.

The Embassy

Your Embassy or Consulate sometimes becomes the focal point for expatriate social life (and the business life as well, in some cases). The facilities of the Embassy – the garden, swimming pool, tennis or squash court or club bar – are frequent venues for diplomatic receptions as well as numerous social, charitable, cultural and commercial functions. Expatriates and their wives are invariably involved in such activities. However, the primary functions of an Embassy are to represent the home Government to the host Government and to protect the interests of its citizens and it must not be regarded as existing largely for the benefit of the expatriate community.

Embassy facilities

Finally, if you are going to stay in a country for any length of time, you should register at the Consul's office in your Embassy.

THE FEMALE EXPATRIATE

The situation of the female expatriate deserves special consideration during the assessment of a post in the region. She needs to be just as adaptable, sensitive and self reliant as her male counterpart, if not more so. If she is a wife and does not have a job then some sort of social activity or interest such as charitable work is essential. The opportunities for employment in what are viewed as appropriate occupations for women expatriates differ from country to country. Nursing and teaching are open to women in all countries, as is secretarial work, except in Saudi Arabia.

Some expatriates choose to move only in their own circles in the Peninsula but a foreign woman certainly does not have to remain isolated from Arab women. Provided she has the opportunity, feels comfortable doing so, and is sufficiently sensitive to the difference in culture, making contact with Arab women can be a most rewarding experience. She is likely to make many firm friends.

On arrival in an Arab country the female expatriate must learn the limits of her freedom. In most countries she will enjoy complete freedom to travel and shop although there will always be male preserves such as coffee houses which are barred to her. In Saudi Arabia, at present, a women may not drive a car and therefore must employ a driver. Furthermore, apart from her driver, a woman in Saudi Arabia may not appear in public accompanied by a man other than her husband or close blood relative such as her father or brother. She is also required to cover her arms and legs and most Saudi Arabian women wear an *abaya* and head shawl. In other countries (and in some cities of Saudi Arabia) the code of behaviour is more relaxed, but there are nevertheless standards of dress applicable to women. (*See* Chapter 1 – *Arab Women* and Chapter 4 – *Standards of Dress*).

A word of warning is necessary concerning relationships with Arab men. The freedom with which Arab men are able to talk to expatriate women is in complete contrast to the relationship which custom

Expatriate women

5

Relationships

5

demands they enjoy with their own womenfolk. Foreign women must be alive to this, behaving with decorum; encouraging the wrong attitude in an Arab male risks offending the Muslim code of conduct.

Islamic law and the Muslim code of conduct strictly forbid relationships outside marriage, whether as partners or extramarital. If such a situation comes to the attention of the authorities, it could well result in deportation, and in some cases imprisonment.

DESERT TRAVEL

One of the most popular recreational pastimes for the expatriate is to visit the remote, unspoiled and beautiful areas of desert, mountains and oases that lie in the hinterland of all the Peninsula countries. Even in the desert, there is a surprising wealth of flora and fauna. However, for the uninitiated the desert can also be a potentially dangerous place. People have become lost, been caught in flash floods and have died from thirst or heat stroke – even on quite short journeys of up to 15 miles. Any forays into the desert must be taken seriously and organised with care. The suitability of your vehicle, its equipment, spares, fuel, water and medical supplies are some of the many considerations. Seek expert advice, take a guide if possible and make sure someone staying behind knows where you have gone and when you are coming back.

Desert
Trekking

Good books on desert travel and camping are on sale in local book shops. Particularly useful is Jim Stabler's *The Desert Driver's Manual* (Stacey International, 1997)

Essential precautions and supplies will include:

- Always take more than one vehicle. Air-conditioned four-wheel drive are best.
- Vehicle equipment of spare wheel (two for long trips), tyre pressure gauge and foot pump, fan belt, tool kit, spare ignition key, spare fuses, tow rope, jack, wooden jacking block, wheel brace, sand channels, shovels, jumper leads, spare oils and fire extinguisher.

- Desert driving uses more fuel than on roads; allow half as much fuel again, plus a reserve.
- Plenty of water and food plus a reserve in case of a breakdown.
- Comprehensive medical kit and knowledge of the treatment for commonly experienced emergencies such as heat stroke (*see* Chapter 4 – *Health Care*).
- Water sterilisation tablets and insect repellent.
- Prior and continued protection against malaria if prevalent in the areas you are visiting.
- Sleeping bags. Even in summer the desert is very cold at night.
- Map, binoculars, compass and a GPS system if you can afford it.
- Mobile phone if coverage is available.
- Knowledge of the desert, as well as desert and mountain driving.
- Rules for travel and camping, e.g. getting lost, avoiding camping in wadis because of flash floods, stagnant water, etc.
- Never travel in a sand storm or at night.
- Beware of camels which stray on to roads and can be difficult to see at dusk and dawn.
- Car insurance cover. International boundaries are not always clear and it is prudent to have cover for both sides of any borders.

5

CHAPTER SIX

·The Business Traveller

INTRODUCTION

The conduct of business in the Peninsula countries may best be summarised as gentlemanly, tricky and time-consuming. The influences at work are rooted in the local culture. Personal relationships are of paramount importance, social and business etiquette must be observed and religion plays a part. Negotiating and striking a deal are conducted on well established lines and the pace is a lot slower than in developed Western countries.

Business etiquette

Today, operating successfully in the Peninsula is a matter of personality and professionalism. Personality amounts to being open, friendly and non-judgmental, able to adapt to the Arab way of doing things, to cope with the heat and frustration and overall, to display a mixture of endless patience and dogged perseverance. Professionalism means efficient market research and business operation and an understanding of the Arab culture, the market and the way business is conducted.

6

THE MARKET

In spite of fluctuations in the price of oil and recent financial crises, this continues to be a long term growth market in both the public and private sectors. It is one of our major trading partners and provides excellent opportunities for exporters of products and services.

The transformation of the infrastructures of the Gulf states in the 1970s was followed by a period of consolidation and the diversification of their economies. The reduction in the oil price at the time was perhaps the beneficial shock that encouraged the move in that direction. But their development continues, with major projects in such fields as oil and gas exploration and production, downstream petrochemicals, power, water management, construction and communications. The traditional markets for defence products, consumer and luxury goods remain and new markets have emerged in tourism, financial services and light industrial

The emerging markets

123

manufacturing. Some of the Peninsula countries have taken a keen interest in agricultural development. Finally, the expansion of the population in the Peninsula states of around 3.5% per annum, with nearly half under the age of 16, continues to fuel the demand for housing, consumer products, healthcare, leisure facilities, education and training (both in-country and overseas).

Niche markets

Current trends characterising the markets in all Gulf states and Saudi Arabia are a move away from public sector financing and towards privatisation, PFI and BOOT projects, and a continued emphasis on Arabisation. For small and medium sized companies approaching this market however, such considerations may not necessarily be relevant. For them it is very often a question of identifying a niche market for their particular product or service.

MARKET RESEARCH

The importance of market research cannot be over-emphasised. It should include a study of:

♦ *The nature/size of the market, principal sectors, demography.*

♦ *Product and service requirements:* What is wanted and why. Gaps in the market. Competition.

♦ *How business is done:* Representatives, agents, joint ventures, stockists.

♦ *The decision-making process:* Who takes the decisions, who influences the decision makers and the procurement system.

♦ *Finance:* Loans, credit, counter-trade agreements, offset.

♦ *Plan of campaign:* A detailed plan of action including estimated timescales.

Assistance with Market Research
In the UK, a company can look to the following organisations and agencies for assistance with market research and support in developing their business:

- UK Trade and Investment (UKTI). This government organisation, part of the Department for Business, Innovation and Skills (BIS), but managed overseas by the Foreign and Commonwealth Office, provides support for both UK companies trading internationally and overseas enterprises seeking to invest in UK. It is sector rather than market oriented. By definition the organisation works closely with the FCO, BIS and other government departments. UKTI contact details: Headquarters Enquiry Service, Kingsgate House, 66-74 Victoria Street, London SW1 6SW Tel: 020 7215 8000. Website: www.uktradeinvest.gov.uk

- The first point of contact for a company registered and based in England would be the International Trade Adviser of UKTI in their regional Business Link office. Business Link is the UK Government's support service for business. Contact details: Tel: 0845 600 9 006
Website: www.businesslink.gov.uk

- Elsewhere in UK Business Link's counterparts in the devolved administrations are:
Scottish Enterprise Tel 0845 609 6611
Website: www.scottishenterprise.com
Wales Trade International. Tel: 029 2080 1046
Website: www.walestrade.com
Invest Northern Ireland Tel: 0 28 9023 9090
Website: www.investni.com

- UKTI International Trade Advisers have expertise in the conduct of business overseas and have specialists in the sectors of industry and the Peninsula markets. UKTI are also represented in all Peninsula countries, including Iraq, based in British Embassies, Consulates General or British Trade Offices. In addition, the devolved administrations have representatives based in UAE.

- The UKTI website contains a wealth of information on the Peninsula countries; country profiles, markets, business practice and regulations and reports on all the main sectors of industry.

UKTI

6

UKTI issue a number of useful business guides and also have a self-service Information Centre.

- UKTI's services include advice and assistance with market research, introductions to overseas markets and opportunities, funding and utilising financial subsidies, export documentation, publicity, promotional material design and publication, and translations.
- Specific UKTI projects currently include:
  - *Passport to Export* programme offering new and inexperienced exporters with the information, expert advice, subsidised training, planning and on-going support they need to succeed in overseas markets.
  - *Gateway to Global Growth*. A free service to experienced exporters which offers reviews, planning and support to help businesses to grow overseas.
  - *Business Opportunities.* Publish specific opportunities for Private Sector sales, joint ventures, investors and partnerships, tenders, and multilateral aid projects across all sectors of industry.
  - *Aid-Funded Business.* Opportunities and advice to businesses.
  - *Market and Sector Research.* An overseas market introduction and research service provided by UKTI's staff at British diplomatic posts overseas. This is fee based but can be subsidised.
  - *Tradeshow Access Programme* This provides grant support for Small and Medium Sized Enterprises (SMEs) to attend and exhibit at key trade shows overseas.
  - *Outward Missions Programme.* Financial support to SMEs for numerous sector and regionally based business visits overseas every year.
- UKTI: Defence and Security Organisation (UKTI DSO) is an integral part of UKTI and provides advice and assistance to the defence and security sectors of UK industry in the promotion of

UKTI DSO

defence and related equipment and services to overseas governments. The directorate of UKTI DSO responsible for the Middle East is Regional Directorate Central. (See contact details below) UKTI DSO also has representatives in a number of UK embassies in Kuwait, Qatar, Saudi Arabia and the UAE. UKTI DSO staff work closely with other government departments including the FCO, MOD and organisations such as the Defence Manufacturers Association (DMA), The Society of British Aerospace Companies (SBAC) and the British Defence Equipment Catalogue Limited. UKTI DSO supports UK industry at a number of defence related exhibitions in UK and overseas. Contact details: UKTI DSO, Regional Directorate Central. Tel: 020 7215 8077.
Website: www.dso.uktradeinvest.gov.uk.

6

♦ Middle East Association (MEA). This is an independent non-profit making organisation financed by its members' subscriptions whose purpose is to promote trade between UK and the Middle East. Membership includes a wide cross section of manufacturing and service industries in UK and overseas (corporate and individual). The MEA is a valuable source of expert information and advice on the Middle East and offers its members a wide range of services towards expanding their business with these markets. Close contact is maintained with government organisations (especially UK Trade and Investment, FCO and MOD) and with UK diplomatic posts in the Middle East as well as with Arab embassies in London. The MEA is involved in organising and managing trade missions to the Middle East, business development conferences in key markets, participating in exhibitions in the region and holding regular receptions for commercial and diplomatic guests and UK Government officials. It also organises frequent seminars and discussion meetings with expert speakers. The Association is a member of bilateral

MEA

trade and economic business councils in Saudi Arabia, Qatar and Dubai. The MEA publishes a fortnightly Information Digest, reports by its staff after visits to the region and the quarterly magazine *Opportunity Middle East*. Contact details: Middle East Association, Bury House, 33 Bury Street, London SWIY 6AX. Tel: 020 7839 2137 Fax: 020 7839 6121. Website www.the-mea.co.uk

- **A-BCC** Arab-British Chamber of Commerce (A-BCC). The A-BCC was founded in 1975 under licence from the then Department of Trade and is devoted to the encouragement and promotion of Arab-British trade and economic co-operation. It provides a wide range of services to Arab and British companies. These include certification and legalisation of documents, business information and research, seminars and workshops on specific countries; visas, translation, language and cultural training, library facilities and a range of business publications. The Chamber works in close co-operation with Arab businesses and legal organisations, particularly the League of Arab States, Arab diplomatic missions in London and Arab and European chambers of commerce. Contact details: The Arab-British Chamber of Commerce, 6 Belgrave Square, London SW1X 8PH. Tel: 020 7235 4363 Fax: 020-7235 1748, website: www.abcc.org.uk

Valuable marketing advice and assistance can also be provided by:

- **Other organisations** Chambers of Commerce. A number of UK Chambers of Commerce have established valuable links with their counterparts in the Peninsula, organise Trade Missions to the region and can often offer expert product and market expertise. They also receive inward delegations and missions from the region.
- Professional trade associations in specialist fields. e.g. the British Consultants and Construction Bureau (BCCB).

- The Commercial Sections of British Embassies, which in addition to personnel from UK Trade and Investment also employ locally engaged staff, often with long service and a wealth of experience of the local market. (*see* Country Annexes for Embassy contact details)

  UK Embassies

- Foreign and Commonwealth Office (FCO). As well as providing indispensable advice on travel, the FCO website has valuable background information reports for all the Peninsula countries and details of diplomatic representation overseas and foreign embassies in UK. Website: www.fco.gov.uk

  FCO

- British Business Groups, who are well established in most countries of the region. (Contact details are given on the UKTI website under Country Profiles).
- Local banks.
- The British Council. On educational and cultural matters. Website www.britishcouncil.org
- Arab Embassies in London (see Country Annexes).
- Offset. Opportunities exist in some Peninsula countries for the establishment of joint venture businesses on beneficial terms as part of offset programmes. Offset is generally required for all major defence contracts, which can be discharged by civil investment such as setting up joint ventures between local companies of the Peninsula country concerned and foreign companies. Civil projects may also increasingly stipulate offset requirements and indeed, as pointed out later in this chapter, contract proposals which feature creative elements for financing, technology transfer and training for local nationals are likely to be particularly welcomed. For opportunities in Saudi Arabia contact the British Offset Office – website: www.britishoffset.com and for other Peninsula countries contact UKTI DSO, UKTI or the Defence Manufacturers Association. Website: www.the-dma.org.uk

  Offset

6

Useful Sources of Information and Publications

- MEED (The Middle East Economic Digest) is recognised as a leading provider of business intelligence to those doing business in or with the Middle East.

MEED

- MEED has an extensive network of journalists and contacts throughout the region and provides an independent and authoritative service to its subscribers – of business news, intelligence, data, analysis and events – in print and online.
- MEED publishes daily news bulletins as well as a range of regular in-depth special reports dealing with all sectors of industry and all the Peninsula countries and Iraq. These cover among other things economic developments, trends, project information, tenders and contract awards and details of key personalities and decision makers.
- MEED also organise a number of regional business events such as international summits and conferences relating to the various sectors of industry.
- MEED contact and subscription details and information on MEED services can be found on their website: www.meed.com which also offers a facility for visitors to subscribe to a free daily news bulletin.

EIU

- The Economist Intelligence Unit (EIU), the business-to-business arm of the Economist Group, is a leading provider of country, industry and management analysis. It has 40 offices worldwide and offers three kinds of business intelligence:
  - Country analysis on more than 200 markets.
  - Industry trends in six key sectors.
  - Latest management strategies and best practices. The EIU provides country reports and country data on all the Peninsular countries and country forecasts on all but Iraq, Oman and Yemen. Details of EIU products and services

and contact details for the four main EUI offices are given on the EUI website: www.eui.com.

- Dun & Bradstreet (D&B). Provide detailed economic information and analysis on all the countries of the region. Their web-based information service covers a wide range of market topics as well as Country Reports (detailed economic analysis), a Country Risk Service (comprehensive information for evaluating risk and opportunities) and two valuable publications – The Exporters Encyclopaedia (annually) and the International Risk and Payment Review (monthly). Contact Details for UK: Tel: 01628 492000 and US: Tel: in-country 800 234 3867 and external 1 (512) 794 7768. Website: www.dnb.com

D&B

- Al Hilal Group in Bahrain are a source of up-to-date business information in the region, posting daily trade and economic news on their website and publishing sector-focussed reports. Website: www.tradearabia.com
- UKTI, MEA, ABCC, British Business Forums in the Gulf countries, local government trade offices and other organisations including those mentioned above produce a wide range of valuable publications on general and specialist business topics on the region such as the 3rd Edition of *Market Essentials Oman*. These are often available free online. Details can be found by searching the Internet or the website of individual organisations such as the BIS website: www.bis.gov.uk/publications.
- *Major Companies of the Arab World* (Edition 32 2009. A comprehensive directory published by Graham and Whiteside. Contact details: Effective Technology Marketing Ltd, PO Box 171, Grimsby UK DN35 OTP. Tel/Fax: (0) 1472 816660 Website: www.dataresources.co.uk

A resume of Department of Commerce support available to US companies wishing to access the Peninsula markets is given on Page 227.

6

PRODUCT REQUIREMENTS

The sales package

When identifying opportunities or gaps in the market, due consideration should be given to what is needed as well as what is wanted. They may not always be the same thing. Some products introduced into the region create more problems than they solve; for example if they require highly skilled operation or complex maintenance. Any sales package therefore should be completely comprehensive and cover installation, training, management, spare parts and maintenance support.

Contracts can be won for a variety of often complex reasons. As a rule, products are attractive if they are the best at the right price and in most cases can be demonstrated to be the latest on the market. They must also be 'proven'. The fact that the product has already been purchased by another prestigious customer or, in the case of Defence equipment, is in service with the British Armed Forces, is an added selling point if not essential. The introduction of a new product, service or technique must take account of traditional and Islamic beliefs. The successful introduction of a new toothpaste acceptable to Muslims, containing no animal fat, is a good example. Finally, attempt to establish what competition (foreign or otherwise) you face in your product range.

There are a number of ways to bring a new product or service to the attention of the Arab market and one should seek advice from UK Trade and Investment in this regard. In particular, UK Trade and Investment offer UK companies a range of subsidised commercial publicity services designed to assist and enhance their export business, especially those participating with UK Trade and Investment support in overseas trade fairs and outward missions.

EXPORT FINANCE AND INSURANCE

Loans and credit

As mentioned, the large imbalance of trade with the West combined with tighter budgets has brought reforms in economic outlook and particularly in the way large projects are financed. Major deals contingent on credit, PFI (Private Finance Initiative), BOOT (build, own, operate and transfer) schemes, counter trade, offset, technology transfer and the formation of joint ventures are increasingly being proposed. It is sensible for foreign companies to consider these requirements at the planning stage. All the advisory organisations mentioned earlier in this chapter under market research can also supply information on funding, i.e. international aid programmes, government loans, extended credit facilities, etc. They will also be aware of banks specialising in various project fields.

Export Credits Guarantee Department (ECGD)

ECGD   **6**

This Government department provides insurance or arranges medium/long-term finance packages in a wide range of markets worldwide for UK exporters of capital goods and projects. ECGD complements insurance available from the private sector which tends to deal with contracts that involve relatively short delivery/credit periods and where contract values are reasonably small. Further information on ECGD support including contact details for private sector companies is to be found on the ECGD website: www.ecgd.gov.uk or telephone London: 020 7512 7000 and Cardiff: 020 2032 8500.

MARKETING PLANS

In the majority of cases the need to establish a personal relationship and mutual trust means that any sales campaign must be staged over a period of time. There will, of course, be notable exceptions – like the salesperson travelling to the Peninsula for the first time as a member of a trade mission with a luxury product for which there was little competition and doubling annual sales in a week! But the successful negotiation of a major export project, perhaps against active competition, is generally a lengthy and often tortuous process, taking months and in some cases years to accomplish. This may be obvious to the experienced business traveller in the region but not to his boss at home, and any sales plan

Thinking
laterally

6

should have a realistic time frame. If the market research is thorough, the Arab decision-maker and those who influence him have been clearly identified and the right people chosen to represent the company, then a visit will not be wasted. You must also always be prepared, however, for business to be concluded in an unorthodox way. Contracts can be won or lost for a wide variety of complicated reasons. Be prepared to think laterally as well as analytically. The preparation and conduct of your visit should take account of the guidelines and advice below.

QUALITIES OF A SUCCESSFUL BUSINESS TRAVELLER

Establishing
a rappport

Two of the qualities necessary for success in the Arab world have been mentioned earlier – endless patience and dogged perseverance. Equally important are the ability to establish a rapport with others at all levels, to have a friendly and open disposition, and show integrity. Finally, it is important to be able to adapt to the way the Arab people do business, behaving with sensitivity towards their culture. The Arab is calm and dignified in his speech and actions and is unfailingly polite. So must you be. Be respectful but not subservient. If necessary, you must be prepared to stand your ground and to refute any unjustified allegation in a calm but diplomatic way and with good humour. The Arabs can be great teasers and do not respect those who rise to the bait or are easily rattled.

The importance attached to personal relationships is very relevant to commercial life. Like you, an Arab will wish to establish whether you can be trusted. This takes time, and the degree of that trust may be directly related to the number of times you have met, but once established, is of great value. *See* Chapter 3 for more information on personal relationships.

Business life in the Arab world is also conducted mainly on the basis of who you know and it pays therefore to get to know as many people as possible. A foreigner will also find he is more readily accepted and trusted if he is open and friendly with everyone he meets. That includes the agent's chauffeur and the client's clerk. It is customary to shake them by the hand on first meeting in the morning and on saying farewell.

It is sometimes said that because the Arabs respect age the older business traveller is likely to be more successful. This is not true. What matters more are the personal qualities described earlier as well as an appreciation of the culture and business methods. As a general rule, the ambitious, go-getting, 'time is money' breed of businessman will not succeed. Although there is a generation of bright young Arab executives coming to the fore in some countries who may follow some of the modern dynamic business methods, they are as yet a minority.

Sometimes an Arab acquaintance will make a personal request which has nothing to do with your commercial dealings. Although this is unusual in our culture, it is wise to try and help.

Finally, an Arab does not like dealing with an underling or with constantly changing faces, a complaint often directed at foreign companies. The person he deals with must have the authority to negotiate without constantly referring to his superiors. Thus an early decision should be taken as to who has the authority to represent a Western

6

Finding the right level

TRUST AS THE BASIS OF BUSINESS

There is the salutary lesson of an Arab client wishing to invest with an English merchant banker whom he knew well and trusted. The Arab visited his friend's bank and offered to invest a large sum of money in whatever his English friend advised. There was no more to be said, but the Englishman decided, for form's sake, to introduce this important new client to his Managing Director. The Managing Director was delighted but, unaware that the deal had been struck on the basis of trust, thought to reinforce the Arab's decision to invest with a short discourse on how successful the bank had been that year. By the end of the speech, the Arab was so suspicious about the Managing Director's need to justify the investment that he withdrew his offer.

6

company for a particular sales campaign and, once appointed, that person should remain the principal point of contact. Since establishing trust is so important, it would be wise to introduce any standby representative at an early stage. Of course, as a project develops it will be necessary for the contact to be at an appropriate level. An Arab Minister, for example, would expect to see the Company Chairman at the proper time.

Businesswomen

Although commerce in the Peninsula is male-dominated, there are nevertheless a number of highly successful Arab businesswomen who control large enterprises although they may personally adopt a low profile. Others conduct business in an exclusively female environment.

Foreign businesswomen have not found it difficult to do business in the region and in several fields they are more successful than men. In the more conservative Arab countries, however, a businesswoman must expect to find that men are sometimes less at ease with her than they would be with a man, although she will always be treated with the utmost courtesy. For her part, the foreign businesswoman should dress soberly, not exaggerate her femininity and, most importantly, she should adopt a polite, straight-forward and businesslike approach without being in any way aggressive or assertive. In Saudi Arabia a businesswoman should be escorted by a local representative or sponsor, who may also be a woman, and she should not forget that in Arabia it is customary for men to walk ahead of women. (*See also* the Country Annex on Saudi Arabia – General Comments.)

One of the best ways for a businesswoman to gain an introduction to the Peninsula market is to participate in an outward trade mission to the region. These are regular events organised by UK Trade and Investment, The MEA, A-BCC and Chambers of Commerce. She may also find it useful to contact Women in Business International (WIB), a not-for-profit company dedicated to supporting women's economic development through its training programmes, international forums and networks. It has been patronised by some very influencial people and organisations making a major contribution in support of businesswomen operating in the Middle East and Asia. The WIB website gives details of events, business resources, expert advisers, publications, training and education. WIB Head Office is in Teddington, UK Tel: +44 (0)20 8943 3630 with a Gulf/Middle East Regional Office in Manama, Bahrain, Enquiries may also be directed to WIB founder Ahmed Suleiman MBE, KFO Tel: + 44 7785 730 409. Website: www.forwomeninbusiness.com.

VISIT ADMINISTRATION

Follow the advice in Chapter 4 – *Visiting The Peninsula.* Additional points for business travellers are set out below.

6

Business Cards

These are normally printed in English on one side and in Arabic on the other. A company logo is best left untranslated but the subtitle beneath, if there is one, should be translated into Arabic. The card may need to be larger than normal to accommodate the Arabic script. It is also worth discussing in detail the meaning that your name and company appointment will have when they are translated to make sure it conveys the correct impression to an Arab customer. You should avoid describing yourself as an 'Assistant' or 'Deputy', even if that is correct in English, as Arab customers do not like to feel that they are dealing with an underling. But also consider how this affects the translation of the cards and titles of any colleagues who may become involved at a later stage. Finally, avoid any obvious misrepresentation. There is a well-known story of a salesman from a large multinational corporation who asked his translator to give him a title that was impressive in Arabic to avoid undue delay in getting to see the right people on his trips to the region. He found he was always given immediate access to the most senior people, but only discovered why later when someone asked him about his role as the President of his corporation.

Dual-language cards

Business Correspondence

It is increasingly common for customers in the region to correspond by fax, e-mail or telephone rather than by letter, but when writing, consider using headed paper with your address in Arabic – the extra expense of having dual English/Arabic language letterhead may well be justified. If a brochure is enclosed it must be in Arabic as well as English. The material should be self-explanatory (no obscure abbreviations), of the highest quality – coloured photographs, maps and diagrams – and not too wordy. For advice on correspondence with Saudi Arabia, see below.

The Western company representative should also be the correspondent with the customer. Nothing is more confusing or annoying to a customer than to receive correspondence from several different people on the same topic. Unfortunately, it is not an uncommon practice, especially in large Western corporations. For legal reasons a Western company may issue a contract under the name of the Commercial Director, for example, but it should be sent to the customer under cover of a letter from the main representative.

Use plain English. Idiomatic and flowery turns of phrase will not be understood or appreciated. Write in the active rather than the passive voice. If any action is being requested in the letter then make a clear statement to that effect, leaving it to the end for emphasis. Finally, in promoting a product or a project, do so in such a way that no criticism is made or implied of any existing system in the Peninsula. (*See also* Chapter 3 – *Forms of Address and Official Correspondence.*)

Translations into Arabic

Documents produced in Arabic are often vital to a sales campaign. In most Peninsula countries brochures should be in English and Arabic and at least the Executive Summary of any proposal should be in both languages. The Arabic and English are usually arranged either alongside one another or with English at the front of the brochure and Arabic at the back. In Saudi Arabia all official correspondence is required by

Letters and brochures

Making yourself clear

6

law to be in Arabic as well as any other language, such as English, and it is advisable to produce separate Arabic and English (or other) documentation.

Good translators are not cheap, partly because they are much in demand and take trouble to impart the true meaning of a document to the reader. Translating documents is usually the last thing one does when preparing for a visit to the region but you will negotiate a better price if you do not ask for a rush job.

Translating documents

A good translator will also advise on the general effect and presentation of any documents and ensure they are relevant to the Arab culture. English trade names, abbreviations and the vernacular, if put directly into Arabic can be meaningless or even offensive. The word '*zip*', for example means 'penis' in Arabic, and a phrase like 'top of the range' would be meaningless if directly translated.

There are several UK firms offering professional translation services and details may be obtained from The Institute of Translation and Interpreting (ITI) who also publish a valuable free guide, *Translating – getting it right*, available on their website: www.iti.org.uk Tel: 01908 325250, Fax: 01908 325259.

6

LOST IN TRANSLATION

What the Arabs see as an over-emphasis on sex in advertisements and the use of peculiarly English puns or colloquialisms do not come across well. A shipment of litter-bins to one Peninsula country turned out to have an inscription describing them as pigs'litters. Simpler mistakes have included a batch of signs which should have warned of camels straying *onto* the road but which showed the camels walking *off* the road – since traffic drives on the right in the Peninsula, the signs are also positioned on the right of the road!

Visit Visas

Passports

Because of the time taken to obtain visas, regular business travellers often apply for an additional passport, and one with extra pages is particularly useful. However, if two passports are used, make absolutely certain that the same passport is always used for the same country. To be discovered using a second passport would present major problems and a possible charge of misrepresentation. It is possible for a frequent traveller to obtain a multi-entry visa. Good travel agents and some chambers of commerce provide a visa service for their members for which they make an administrative charge.

Entry visas

Some countries have special entry requirements. For Saudi Arabia, for example, a visa application must be accompanied by a letter of invitation from a Saudi sponsor. Regulations of this sort vary from country to country and are, of course, liable to change. *See* Chapter 4 and the Country Annexes for further details.

Dress and General Appearance

Pay attention to your appearance – you will be judged on how you look. A businessman should be smartly but soberly dressed – a good-quality suit (lightweight in summer). If a jacket is not worn, a long sleeved shirt and tie are appropriate. Businesswomen should dress modestly in loose fitting clothes that cover the arms and legs and come up to the neck. (*See also* General Comments in the Country Annex on Saudi Arabia.)

Security During Overseas Visits

As mentioned, although Arab countries are traditionally safe places to visit, the current threat from terrorism, including attacks on Westerners, means that visitors to the region must give serious attention to their personal security. In addition to the valuable advice given on the FCO website, the business traveller can also obtain guidance from the FCO's Security Information Service for Businesses Overseas (SISBO). Details of this service are given on the FCO website: www.fco.gov.uk and/or contact the Business Team in the Global Business Group of FCO: Email: peter.obrien@fco.gov.uk or telephone 020 7008 3675. SISBO co-ordinators are located in all British embassies overseas.

Business Samples
Business samples are best accompanied by a certificate explaining that they are of no commercial value and are being carried as an essential part of your work.

PREPARATION AND TIMING OF A VISIT TO THE REGION

In addition to the advice given in Chapter 4, plans should take account of:

6

- Appropriate preparatory action having been taken by a local agent, the Commercial Officer or the Defence Attaché (in the case of Defence sales) of your Embassy, if you have enlisted their help.
- The availability of all those you wish to see; Arab clients, agents, British Ambassador, Commercial Officer or Defence Attaché, etc.
- The time of year. The summer months of July and August and school holidays tend to be times when Arab customers take holidays abroad, and the hotter months are generally less conducive to doing business.
- The holy month of the fast of Ramadan is best avoided. Working hours are curtailed, particularly towards the end of this month. The dates, which are different each year by the Western calendar, are forecast at the end of Chapter 1.
- The main Muslim festivals are also best avoided if they are holidays in the country you are visiting. In Saudi Arabia only the *Eid Al-Adha* and *Eid Al-Fitr* are celebrated as holidays. The dates, which again change each year are also forecast in Chapter 1.
- National Days (dates are given in the Country Annexes). Also note any holiday observed by Embassies, such as the British Embassy's Queen's Birthday celebrations.

Choosing the right adviser

141

- The Pilgrimage. Flights to the region and particularly to and within Saudi Arabia can be very crowded during the period of the run up to, and end of, the annual Hajj pilgrimage.
- Consider the working week and business hours. For details see Chapter 1 and the Country Annexes.

THE CONDUCT OF BUSINESS

The Embassy

The first port of call, unless you have been advised otherwise, and particularly on your initial visit to a country, will probably be the Embassy. This is not only a basic courtesy but good sense as their assistance and advice can be invaluable. It may be best not to highlight any link with the Embassy to your Arab customer until you are sure of his attitude, in case it offends his sense of confidentiality.

The Commercial Section of the Embassy exists to promote trade. An Ambassador holds frequent receptions for visiting trade missions or important commercial initiatives to which he will invite influential local dignitaries, heads of industry and commerce, and local businessmen. The Commercial Officer, his staff and the Defence Attaché will also be involved. Such functions can provide invaluable access to local businessmen and the decision-makers.

Local Agents, Sponsors, Consultants and Advisers

Local Agents

Large numbers of agents, sponsors and consultants operate in the Peninsula, their role being to facilitate transactions between foreign businessmen and their customers. They are paid a fixed fee or a percentage of any business and their services usually amount to the promotion of goods to local customers, identifying market opportunities and gaining access to the decision-makers. This system, although strange and even repugnant to some Westerners, is a legitimate and often essential business practice in the region. Any business traveller who has spent countless hours in the outer office of a Shaikh or waited for days in a hotel for a telephone response, is grateful for it. What is not to be countenanced is the man who, hearing of a contract in the offing, threatens to spoil it unless he is cut in on the deal; i.e. he claims the ability to bring the deal to a successful conclusion, with the clear implication that without him the deal won't go through. This is a difficult situation which must be dealt with in the light of the circumstances but your agents, consultants, professional bodies or local Embassy will provide good advice.

Never confuse the payment to an agent or consultant for legitimate business services with a bribe. You may hear a number of stories about bribery and corruption and it may be suggested that such practices occasionally oil the wheels, but bribery is a serious offence in all states of the region and the penalties are severe.

6

Agent's fees

Although it is usual to use sponsors and local representatives it is not always obligatory and it is even forbidden for certain types of business. Nevertheless, most Western companies feel the need for a local adviser of some kind and they usually make a major contribution to success. The problem invariably lies in choosing the right one. It is an important and tricky subject and one on which a businessman should get as much good advice as he can before committing himself.

The type of arrangement you make will depend on the nature of your business. Regulations on the necessity for sponsors and agents or otherwise vary from country to country and depend on whether for example, you are exporting, setting up a representative office, business or joint venture operation and who is the customer. If you are involved in the latter two activities then a sponsor is likely to be obligatory. For some Western exports it would not be essential and in the field of Defence it is expressly forbidden and companies awarded a contract are asked to sign a statement to the effect that no commission has been paid to a third party. Information on regulations concerning local representation, agents and distributors in each Peninsula country is given on the UK Trade &

Commission

6

Investment website: www.uktradeinvest.gov.uk. It is advisable to visit a local lawyer at an early stage in any campaign and obtain a briefing on the options available and the legal and other implications of each option. Your embassy and local lawyers are usually well briefed in these matters. If agents are expressly forbidden in any field or for any other reason it is never worth trying to get round the law.

Thoroughly research the suitability of an agent and be as certain as possible that he has the necessary influence to ensure access, can obtain a favourable response from the decision-makers, and can provide good market intelligence including information on the competition, before signing up with him. These are the main requirements of a good agent and it is prudent to have some proof of his effectiveness from himself and others. Asking a third party about him calls for discretion. He may have a record of success but can he sustain it? Any agreement with an agent should be drawn up in writing which must be fair to both sides. He will want you to make enough of a commitment to justify his efforts and you will want to safeguard yourself against an ineffective agent. The agreement should specify the field of operation in detail and have a time limit if possible. In some countries and in some circumstances it is extremely difficult to sack an ineffective agent once he has been appointed and local court cases can be expensive, embarrassing and detrimental to one's business.

Finally, although it might appear to the newcomer to the Arab scene that progress without local help is impossible, and agents do often have an important role to play, their activities should never be allowed to become a substitute for your own direct contact with the customer.

The Decision-making Process

Decision
making

The decision-making process, particularly in the public sector, is often dominated by a small number of powerful individuals. Authority to take decisions may not be delegated in our bureaucratic way but all decisions, large and small, are often referred back to the top. This has the advantage on occasions that major decisions are taken remarkably quickly and with the minimum of fuss.

However, the decision-makers also rely on the increasing use of expert consultants, advisory committees and boards, not only for major projects but also for product purchase. A formalised system of procurement is an established feature of all the Peninsula Defence Forces, large entities such as national oil companies and most departments of government. You are likely, therefore, to have the effectiveness and value of your product examined by a number of highly competent experts and government officials who then report on it to the decision-maker. One of the important aims of market research is to ascertain who makes the final decision.

Middle management

Dealing with commercial firms is slightly different. The centuries-long tradition of trade in the Arab world has brought certain families to prominence. The private sector is still largely dominated by family business. The heads of these large trading families, are much respected figures of the establishment and again the decision-making is confined to relatively few people.

Middle management has an important role to play and should not be ignored or consciously bypassed. Bear in mind that a special feature of the region is that a strong bond of loyalty links the middle manager to his boss. This bond will be strengthened rather than weakened if the middle manager is an Arab expatriate. In Saudi Arabia and some of the Gulf States many of them will be Lebanese, Egyptian or Palestinian by origin.

Access

One particular hurdle for any international businessman is gaining access to the decision-makers. In spite of the traditional custom of approachability – or perhaps because of it – it is often difficult for a foreigner to do this and the more senior the person the more difficult the access. It is generally far too time-consuming to work one's way up. The organisations mentioned above under Market Research will usually give good advice. Often your local Embassy can help, the Defence Attaché in the

6

6

case of Defence products or the Commercial Counsellor in the commercial field.

In the case of Defence products, the Defence Attaché will advise (and update) you on the procurement process, staff lists, locations of military personnel and security regulations and procedures which you are likely to encounter when dealing with the military in a particular Peninsula country. In the commercial field Western companies usually employ the services of a sponsor or agent, which is generally not permitted in the field of defence sales.

Defence sales

Whatever assistance you receive, access is always a problem. Because the decision-making process is centralised in a few hands, the decision-makers are much in demand not only from foreign visitors but also those both above and below them.A minister may be sent for by a ruler at short notice and detained, sometimes for an extended period. An Arab's commitment to his family or friends may make similar demands on his time. In spite of the fact that the pace of life is ever quickening, Arabs do not naturally make appointments to see each other on a routine basis and do not like to plan their schedules too tightly or too far into the future. It is therefore not sensible for a foreign visitor to request an appointment more than say a week or so in advance or to be inflexible over the date or timing if something should force a change. Having said that, if the request for access is clearly beneficial to an Arab as well as the visitor an Arab will often go out of his way to grant it.

Appointments

Confidentiality
As a basic principle it is always best to keep your dealings strictly confidential. In an area where competition is keen and everyone is intensely interested in everyone else's business an Arab customer will expect you to obey what is sometimes termed 'The Third Party Rule', i.e. never repeat to a third party what an Arab has told you. Also avoid mentioning to an Arab what someone has said to you, or he may think you are repeating what he says in the same way.

Third Party Rule

Business Etiquette

Follow closely the general advice given in Chapter 3. If you are invited to mention the subject of your visit during an initial meeting and other people are present, give only enough information to interest the Arab in granting you an exclusive interview at a later date when the matter may be discussed in more detail. He may well suggest the venue or he may accept an invitation to a meal in a local hotel, perhaps in a private room or, failing that, to discuss matters with one of his trusted subordinates.

Formal Presentations

Any presentation in this highly competitive market must be efficiently produced and take into consideration the following:

6

Presentations

- ◆ Language. Most presentations in the region are given in English but if it is clear that it would be better to communicate in Arabic choose a good interpreter. It is usually possible to hire someone locally. He should be intelligent enough to earn the respect of the Arab customer and speak in an acceptable dialect, i.e. either the local dialect of the country you are in or classical Arabic. Egyptian and Palestinian Arabic is universally understood. If the presentation is in English then follow the advice on Communication given in Chapter 3.
- ◆ Rehearse well. Keep it straightforward with the minimum of abbreviations and mnemonics.
- ◆ Take it slowly, allow questions during your dialogue and pauses for customer participation.
- ◆ The script of the presentation (attractively bound) may also be provided for the clients – in Arabic and English together with a copy of any audio-visual material.
- ◆ The presentation should be short – say 20 minutes, with time for questions.
- ◆ Do not imply criticism of any existing facility or organisation when plugging your own product.
- ◆ Brochures should be produced to a high standard. Follow the advice under 'Translations into Arabic' above. Technical data is best put in an annex to any document.

147

Demonstrations

Demonstrations and Trials

It is best to establish at the planning stage of any project whether a demonstration or trial will be necessary. They are however, often extremely time-consuming and costly. (Will the customer contribute?) A successful demonstration, particularly of defence equipment, calls for the highest degree of professionalism. The following matters should be addressed:

- Several rehearsals under conditions identical to the final demonstration. Anticipate everything that could go wrong.
- A backup or duplicate at every stage to replace anything that does go wrong.
- Simplicity of presentation.
- Translated speech in the dialect of the Arab customer.
- An illustrated written record of the demonstration.
- A film or video to augment the demonstration (perhaps including any feature that could not, for safety reasons, be demonstrated).
- Use local Arab operators but make sure they are trained, rehearsed and controlled.
- Availability of the decision-makers and their attendance.
- That extra idea to make an impact.
- A memento of the occasion as a gift to the principal person or persons present.

Promotional Gifts

As in any commercial dealings, promotional gifts such as diaries and calendars, (which can be produced including the Hejirian* dates), pens or paperweights, and other gifts are sometimes appropriate and may serve to keep a firm's name prominent in the client's mind. Gifts should always be carefully chosen to reflect the relative importance of the recipient, e.g. the Arab Director General of an Organisation should be given a more prestigious gift than a member of his staff. It is wise to

See page 37 – Nicholas Smith Internatioal Ltd

record the giving as it is often difficult to remember a year later what you gave and when. It should also be remembered that gifts need to be matched to the recipient. In countries such as the Gulf states where luxury goods are commonplace the expense of a gift to a senior citizen or Shaikh can be considerable. It would be better to do it properly or not at all. A newcomer should seek advice from an experienced colleague.

Subsequent Visits and Refusals

The rule is to visit often. Arabs are justifiably cynical about single visits and the apparent lack of a commitment on the part of the Western businessman. Arab courtesy is such that you will not usually receive a directly negative response to a business proposal. If you have failed to get a response and the Arab in question has clearly had every opportunity to give one, then you have to be able to recognise the signs that clearly point in the direction of rejection or a change of circumstances (which can amount to the same thing). All too often one hears of the frustrated foreigner who says 'I have heard absolutely nothing. I have no idea what they think!' But if you suspect you have failed, it is not a good idea to embarrass an Arab by pressing him to clarify his position.

Negotiations

As has been said in Chapter 3 under *Bargaining*, foreigners often find bargaining tedious, but to the Arabs of this part of the world it is second nature and is bound to be a feature of any business deal. It is wise to be well prepared. It should be approached as the art of compromise without backing down or losing face. To negotiate a good deal is a matter of pride to an Arab and it will be very important to achieve it if he is dealing on behalf of himself, his organisation or his Government. This being the case, for you to make a significant reduction in price during a negotiation without reason (as sadly is sometimes done) is to encourage the belief that you were significantly overcharging. Therefore at each stage of a negotiation there must be a meaningful

Leaving room for manouevre

149

6

reason for reducing a price or changing a position. Plan at the outset to leave room to manoeuvre in any contract, both for reducing the price a number of times (perhaps by removing optional elements) or to offer some added attractions to compensate for sticking at your original price. Always try to keep something in reserve because it will certainly be needed!

Negotiations can be tough, heated and with unusually forthright statements being made by the Arab customer, some of which may shock you. In some instances this is a deliberate negotiating technique. Keep your cool, firmly refute any unjustified statement and, above all, do not allow any altercation to become personal.

Listening to the customer

As well as striving to maintain a pleasant relationship with an Arab customer it is important to be especially sensitive and responsive to what he says during your dealings. He may sometimes give you genuinely helpful advice. He may do this obliquely. In doing so he may be compensating for the gap in culture and understanding between you and because he likes you. The words may sometimes be intended for your ears only. It has happened more than once in my experience and it pays to listen very carefully to what he says – such hints are often missed.

Verbal Agreements and Records of Meetings

Arab memory

There is a strong tradition in the Arab world of concluding agreements verbally. Modern bureaucracy demands that they now be put in writing, but even today some Arabs will regard an oral agreement as binding. Arabs pride themselves on having prodigious memories for every detail in even the most protracted negotiations and it is very important not to make an oral commitment or a promise that you cannot keep. It is always sensible to write to an Arab customer following a meeting, thanking him and at the same time confirming your understanding of any important conversation or decision. Although it is often tiresome to do so, it confirms the situation to both parties, flushes out any misunderstandings and prevents any change of mind which one side or the other could later seek to introduce.

It is wise to be aware of the Arab characteristic of adhering to the letter of any agreement as well as to the spirit of it. If both sides have established a genuine rapport, however, then written agreements are usually consigned to the filing cabinet and the parties proceed on the basis of mutual trust, a situation much preferred in Peninsula countries.

Contracts

Advice on the content of contracts can be obtained from your company or local lawyer, the Embassy Commercial Section or from UK Trade and Investment. Whereas a Western company may wish a contract to conform to the laws of its home country, this may not be acceptable to the Arab customer who may wish his own jurisdiction to apply. It is sensible for foreign companies to take both home-based and local legal advice for large contracts to safeguard their interests, although they may sometimes have to accept that this may not be entirely to the extent that they would wish.

Legal assistance

In all the capitals of the Peninsula countries there are representative offices of leading Western legal firms, generally in partnership with local firms. There are also excellent local firms. Many have extensive experience in commercial contract work as well as the formation of joint ventures, BOOT, private finance, counter trade and offset etc.

As a general principle contracts should be kept as simple as possible. The language must be straight-forward, bearing in mind that it will be translated into

6

Export
licences

Arabic. For clarity, use short sentences and relegate detailed or technical data to an annex. Finally, avoid introducing later amendments, or your integrity may be called into question!

Licences
The export of certain goods, including technology, is subject to export control and the granting of a government licence and advice is best sought at an early stage in any marketing campaign. The control and licensing of products for export is the responsibility of the Export Control Organisation (ECO) of the Department for Business, Innovation and Skills (BIS). ECO can provide advice on establishing whether or not specific goods need an export licence, the different types of licence, how to apply and how long they take to process. This information can be accessed on their website: www.berr.gov.uk/exportcontrol or by contacting ECO on: ECO.Help@berr.gsi.gov.uk Tel: 020 7215 4594. UKTI DSO (see page 126) can provide information concerning the export of defence related equipment.

Western VIP Visits to the Arab World
The business traveller should ensure that any senior executive of his or her company who visits the Arab world is well briefed on the customs of the region. There is more than one story of a senior businessman flying out to clinch an important contract, who unwittingly commits a *faux pas* with an Arab official or ruler and suddenly finds, inexplicably, that the deal is not confirmed.

The VIP should be made aware in particular of the importance of personal relationships in commerce. The fact, for example, that one reason for winning a contract will be that the Arab customer likes and trusts the person who has been representing the company.

Finally, the visiting VIP should be warned of the necessity for extreme flexibility with his programme, and that nobody can visit the region on a tight schedule with guaranteed appointments.

Islamic Attitudes to Commerce

It is as well to be aware of the Islamic view of commerce. The writings of the Holy Quran look with favour on commercial activity. It specifically condemns fraudulent practice. Unlike Christianity, however, nothing is said against the accumulation of wealth and possessions (Arabs traditionally dislike anyone who boasts of a lack of them), but Islam does lay a duty on the rich to use their wealth for the common good and specifically to give alms (*zakat*) to the poor. *See* Chapter 1, *Islam*.

Islam and commerce

The writings of the Holy Quran are also clearly opposed to any gain accruing from chance, and usury is expressly forbidden. These beliefs have been interpreted to take account of modern commercial practice. Insurance was also originally frowned upon by orthodox Islamic opinion because it was seen as an attempt to frustrate the will of God – if God wills a man to suffer loss, he must do so and not seek compensation. However, the huge sums invested in projects today have made such a strict interpretation impractical.

6

A local lawyer will advise on the extent to which the *Sharia* law applies to any dealings in the Peninsula.

Entertaining an Arab Customer in UK

Follow the advice given in Chapter 3 under *Entertainment*. In addition, if you invite an Arab client to the UK it is important to make it clear what your invitation entails. The value of the exercise might be totally negated if there is, for example, a misunderstanding as to who pays what bill. Some commercial companies might invite an Arab client to London, offering to pay the air fare and/or the hotel bill, together with all transportation and entertainment for a specified period and leave it to the client to stay on longer at his own expense if he or she wishes. You might also consider asking the client if he/she would mind settling their own telephone bill. Finally, you should confirm that the hotel understands what it means to cater for the needs of a Muslim guest. Most large London hotels are fully aware of the requirements, but provincial hotels may not be.

Be as generous in your hospitality as your Arab guest would undoubtedly be if he were the host. If the visit is to London, then one of the modern luxury hotels would be appropriate accommodation. If feasible, you should allocate a private Prayer Room at each venue for your guest together with a compass to indicate the direction of Makkah and quietly inform your guest that this is available if required.

The schedule should not be too crowded. Allow some time for relaxation, sightseeing and shopping and possibly a private social engagement.

Follow the advice given in Chapter 3 under *Receiving an Arab* and *Entertaining*.

Annexes

Regional Organisations

The Arab League

Formed in 1945, The Arab League exists to co-ordinate policies and activities towards the common good of all Arab states. All the Arab states of North Africa and the Middle East are members including those of the Arabian Peninsula. A large number of committees attached to the council deal with a variety of sectors of interest to the League such as political, economic, cultural, social, financial and legal affairs. The Arab Monetary Fund set up by the League in 1977 provides financial assistance to member states. The permanent headquarters is based in Cairo and the League has representative offices in a number of Western countries and at the United Nations.

The Gulf Co-operation Council (GCC)

The GCC is a council of six of the Peninsula countries: the Kingdoms of Saudi Arabia and Bahrain, the States of Kuwait and Qatar, the United Arab Emirates and Oman, It was formed in 1981 to strenghten relations between its members and to co-ordinate and unify policies in all fields including politics, economics and defence. It is the vehicle for establishing common systems in the GCC in such areas as finance, education, communications, travel, legal, customs and trade affairs. Its permanent headquarters is in Riyadh, Saudi Arabia.

The Organisation of Arab Petroleum Exporting Countries (OAPEC)

The Kingdoms of Saudi Arabia and Bahrain, the States of Kuwait and Qatar, the United Arab Emirates and the Republic of Iraq and other Arab oil producing countries of the Middle East formed this organisation in 1968 with its headquarters in Kuwait. Its aims are to safeguard the

GCC

OAPEC

interests of its members and organise co-operation in
various fields of the petroleum industry.

OPEC

Note 1: Saudi Arabia, the UAE, Qatar, Kuwait and Iraq are also
members of the wider grouping the Organisation of Petroleum
Exporting Countries (OPEC).

OIC

Note 2: All the Peninsula States are also members of the Organisation
of The Islamic Conference (OIC) of Islamic nations whose Secretariat is
based in Jeddah, Saudi Arabia and which promotes Islamic values and
among other activities provides aid to Muslim communities in need.

REGIONAL ORGANISATIONS

The Kingdom of Bahrain

Geography

The island Kingdom of Bahrain, situated midway down the Arab Gulf about 29 kms from the coast of Saudi Arabia, consists of an archipelago of 33 low-lying islands with a total area of 665 sq kms. The largest island, also called Bahrain, is about 50 kms long and 16 kms wide. Manama, the capital city and main commercial centre is linked to the second largest town and international airport, Muharraq, by a causeway and bridge. Another causeway links Bahrain with mainland Saudi Arabia and a further causeway planned linking Bahrain with Qatar. The main port is Mina Salman. Industrial development is concentrated on Sitra Island. Other major towns are Rifa'a, Isa Town and Awali. A major new financial centre 'Bahrian Financial Harbour' is under construction on the north coast of Bahrain and a large tourist development 'Durrat Al-Bahrain', similar to Dubai's Palm Island is under construction off the southeast tip of Bahrain.

Climate

Pleasant from November to March, warm by day and cool by night with temperatures varying between 14 and 24°C. From May to October it can be extremely hot and humid with temperatures averaging 36°C by day.

History

In ancient history, Bahrain (in Arabic meaning 'two seas') was the site of Dilmun and part of a great civilisation and trading empire. As well as having a strong trading heritage the island was known for its lush vegetation, plentiful sweet water and pearls. One of the first territories outside the Arab mainland to accept Islam, it later formed part of the Umayyad and Abbasid empires and thereafter was frequently fought over by a succession of powers seeking

B
A
H
R
A
I
N

influence in the Arab Gulf. Following Britain's withdrawal from the region the country declared full independence in 1971. A constitution was introduced in 1973 which provided for a democratic National Assembly but this was dissolved in 1975. However, since 1999 major reforms have introduced a new constitution and transformed Bahrain's system of government.

Government

Bahrain is a hereditary constitutional monarchy. His Majesty the King, Shaikh Hamad bin Isa Al-Khalifa is a member of the Al-Khalifa family which has ruled the country since 1783. Since his succession in 1999, Shaikh Hamad has instituted a number of major political reforms, initiating the drawing up of a National Action Charter (NAC), abolishing the State Security Law and pardoning political prisoners. In 2002 the NAC led to the introduction a new constitution, transforming Bahrain into a hereditary constitutional monarchy with a bi-cameral parliamentary system of a National Assembly, comprising a lower elected chamber and an appointed upper (consultative) chamber. Elections to the National Assembly were held in the same year.

Economy

With less dependence on oil than other Gulf states, Bahrain has succeeded in diversifying its economy. Major industries are aluminium smelting, oil refining, financial services (particularly Islamic banking), human resources development and training, and tourism. There are two free zones at north Sitra and Mina Sulman. Bahrainisation is a high government priority. Overall the economic environment is liberal and well regulated. Although it is not obligatory, goods are normally sold through a local agent.

Population

Approximately 698,500 including over 230,000 expatriates, concentrated mainly in the north around the capital, Manama. Projected Bahraini National growth rate is 1.6%

per annum. Most Bahraini Nationals are Arabs but a large number are also of Iranian ancestry.

Religion
The state religion is Islam, 85% of the population being Muslim, approximately two thirds Shia and one third Sunni. The ruling family and many of the leading merchant families are Sunni. There are also indigenous Christian, Jewish, Hindu, Parsee and other minorities.

Official Language
Arabic. English is widely spoken in business and official circles and by expatriates working in the service sector.

National Flag
Currently red with a broad serrated white stripe along the hoist, the national flag is to be replaced by a new design of five triangles representing the five pillars of Islam.

Visas
UK nationals may purchase a three-month visa on arrival at Bahrain International Airport (Cost: BD 5.00). Alternatively, a six-month visa may be obtained prior to travelling from the Bahrain Embassy in London (*see* below). Similarly, US citizens can purchase a three day/one week visa on arrival or a longer period visa may be obtained prior to travelling from the Bahrain Embassy in Washington DC (*see* below). Visas may be extended in Bahrain. Penalties for overstaying can be costly. Passports should be valid for at least six months on arrival. Video cassettes should not be carried as they may be withdrawn at the airport. There is an Airport Departure Tax of BD 3.00. Consult current travel regulations published on the FCO website before travel.

Alcohol
Non-Muslims may import up to one litre of wine of spirits or six cans of beer duty free. Alcohol is available for non-Muslims in certain hotels, and may be purchased

Local Time GMT + 3 hours, EST + 8 hours

Dialling Code 973. All fixed lines commence with 17 and mobile numbers with 3.

Public Holidays
All Muslim Festivals (*see* Chapter 1); New Year's Day – 1 January and National Day – 16th December.

Working Hours (local time)
Government offices: 0700-1415 Saturday to Wednesday.
Banks: 0730-1200 and 1530-1730 Saturday to Wednesday; 0700-1100 on Thursday. Business hours: either 0800-1530 Saturday to Wednesday or 0800-1300 and 1500-1730 Saturday to Wednesday.
Shops: 0830/0900-1230 and 1530-1730 Saturday to Thursday with extended hours for superstores, shopping malls and the *sooq*.
British Embassy: 0730-1430 Sunday to Thursday.
The working week and working hours are sometimes extensively amended during the holy month of Ramadan.

Currency
Bahraini Dinar (BHD) divided into 1,000 Fils. At the time of going to print, the exchange rate was BHD .613 = £1 sterling and linked to the US$ at BHD .38 = US $1. Credit cards are widely accepted and most major banks are linked to at least one international ATM network.

Income Tax
There is no personal taxation.

Electricity Supply
230 volts, except Awali town which uses 110 volts. There are various plug fittings usually three-pin flat type.

Transportation
Most hotels have an airport pick up service on arrival in Bahrain. Taxis have meters. Check that they are set before

for 3 months and indefinitely on an international licence. The national airline is Gulf Air owned jointly by Bahrain, Abu Dhabi (UAE) and Oman.

Tipping
Taxis – tips appreciated. Hotels normally add 15% service charge (as do restaurants) and a 5% tax to their bills. Tips in such cases not expected. Airport porters, 100 fils per item of baggage.

Embassies
Embassy of the Kingdom of Bahrain in UK
30 Belgrave Square, London SW1X 8QB.
Tel: 0207 201 9170. *Opening Hours: 09.00am-3.00pm.*
Embassy of the State of Bahrain in the US:
3502 International Drive NW, Washington DC 20008
Tel: 202 342 0741.
British Embassy in Bahrain:
21 Government Avenue, Manama 306.
Postal address: PO Box 114, Manama, Kingdom of Bahrain. Tel: 00 973 17574100
Website: https//ukinbahrain.fco.gov.uk;
US Embassy in Bahrain:
Shaikh Isa Bin Salman Highway, Al-Zinj District, Manama. Tel: 00 973 17273 300.
Website: https://bahrain.usembassy.gov

Tourist Sites
Sites include the National Museum on Al-Fateh Highway; the Heritage Centre and the Museum of Pearl Diving on Government Avenue; Wind Towers (several locations); Bab-Al-Bahrain (City gateway); the *Sooq*, Beit Al-Quran (Museum and Research Centre) (obligatory to dress conservatively) off Exhibition Avenue; The Friday Mosque on Al-Khalifa Avenue; the Dhow Building Yards near Pearl Monument roundabout; Al-Fatih Mosque on Al-Fatih Highway (shorts not permitted; women are given, and expected to wear, an *abaya*) and the Bahrain Craft Centre on Isa Al-Kabeer Avenue. Al-'Areen Wildlife Sanctuary (controlled access).

General Comments

Although Bahrain is a very liberal country by Arab Gulf standards, it is nevertheless a very conservative society. Visitors should dress soberly, particularly in public places and in rural areas. When visiting mosques it is obligatory to remove one's shoes and women are expected to cover their heads. As in all Gulf countries, care should be exercised with photography, obtain permission when photographing men and do not photograph women.

Further Information

FCO Country Profile and Travel Advice: www.fco.gov.uk
UK Trade & Investment Country Profile:
www.uktradeinvest.gov.uk
Lonely Planet *Oman, UAE & Arabian Peninsula Travel Guide* ISBN: 9781741045468

B
A
H
R
A
I
N

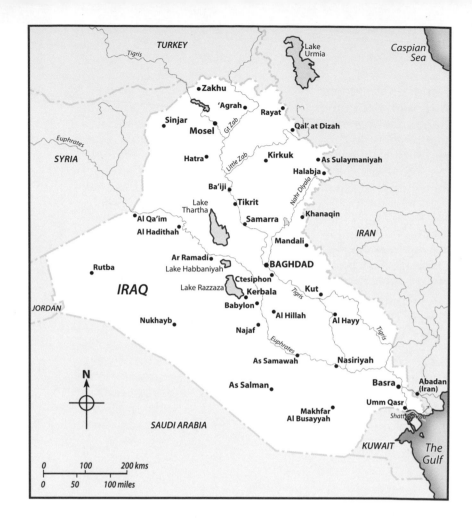

The Republic of Iraq

Geography

The Republic of Iraq extends northwest from the head of the Gulf and covers an area of 437,072 sq km. It is bounded by Turkey, Iran, Kuwait, Saudi Arabia, Jordan and Syria. A short 56 km coastline gives it access to the Gulf. It has four distinct topographical regions. The first, the upper plain in the northwest, bordering Syria, is a fertile area lying between the Euphrates and Tigris rivers, whose chief cities are Mosul and Kirkuk. The second, in the far northeast above Kirkuk (and part of Kurdistan), bordering Turkey and Iran, is a mountainous area rising at its highest point, Mount Halgurd, to 3,728m. The third is the low lying plain extending south-eastwards from the capital Baghdad, encompassing the lower reaches of the Euphrates and the Tigris, which then combine to become the wide Shatt Al-Arab waterway that flows through Basra (Iraq's main port), to the Gulf. The fourth region is the extensive western desert, stretching to the borders of Kuwait, Saudi Arabia, Jordan and Syria.

Climate

In summer (May to September) Iraq is hot with average temperatures of 34°C in Baghdad and 37°C in Basra. In the hottest months (July and August) temperatures of well over 40°C are common. There is high humidity in the south and dust storms occur in the central plains. In the north it is cooler. In winter, the average temperature in Baghdad is 11°C and in Basra 14°C. However, in the mountains of north-eastern Iraq it is cold and there is snow. Except in the northeast, rainfall, which occurs in the winter months, is sparse.

History

Historically known as Mesopotamia, from the Greek 'between two rivers', the land between the Tigris and the Euphrates (and now part of modern Iraq) is steeped in history. In ancient times is was the site of some of the world's greatest civilizations and from the 8th to 13th Century, Baghdad was the seat of the second dynasty of the Islamic Empire, the Abbasid Caliphate. From the 17th Century the territory was ruled by the Ottoman Turks until the First World War when it came under British mandate and in 1932 became an independent monarchy. However, on 14th July 1958 the monarchy was overthrown in a military coup and Iraq declared a republic. There followed a series of coups and counter-coups although a period of stability in the 1970s allowed Iraq to derive considerable benefit from its large oil resources.

In 1979 Saddam Hussain came to power at the head of a minority Sunni regime. Under his rule, Iraq suffered almost continuous internal and external conflict, enormous loss of life and the almost total devastation of its economy and infrastructure. Saddam's regime saw Iran as a constant threat which, allied to Iraq's majority Shia population who are located mostly in the south, sought to destabilise or overthrow it. In 1980, under the pretext of a dispute over the sovereignty of the Shatt Al-Arab waterway, Saddam launched an attack on Iran. The resultant war lasted for eight years and cost over a million lives on both sides. In the same year, in response to Kurdish guerrilla activities in the north of the country, the regime took brutal reprisals (including the use of chemical weapons at Halabja) against Iraq's Kurdish population.

In 1990, Saddam invaded and occupied Kuwait, again under a pretext – this time claiming sovereignty over Kuwait and its oil-fields but in 1991, US-led Coalition forces (including a strong UK component) expelled the Iraqis, driving them back towards Baghdad. In the aftermath, there were renewed uprisings in the Shia populated south and in the Kurdish north which were again brutally repressed with huge loss of life and a mass exodus of refugees. Iraq was placed under sweeping and stringent UN sanctions and controls which Saddam continually exploited and flouted.

This led, in 2003, to the US/UK and coalition military action which overthrew Saddam and his regime. Since then, the US, UK and coalition forces have provided extensive military support to maintain internal stability in Iraq and the international community have contributed massive funding and assistance for the reconstruction of the political, economic and social life of the country. At the time of going to press the timetable for the troop withdrawal is well advanced, the remaining US forces having handed over control of security to the new Iraqi government and will in future only take part in military operations at the request of the Iraqi authorities. Although an enormous amount has been achieved in the reconstruction of the country it still has a long way to go to stabilise the internal security situation, reconstruct the economy and provide an environment in which normal social life can be resumed.

Population and Religion
Estimated at 24.6 million, of which 4 million live in Baghdad, 2 million in Basra and 1.5 million in Mosul. The distribution of the population is 17% Sunni Kurds concentrated in the northeast of the country, 20% Sunni Arabs mainly in the central region and 60% Shia Arabs concentrated mainly in the south. Karbala and Najaf (Al-Najaf) are two of the most important Shia shrines. There are also small groups of Turkomans, Assyrians and Armenians, Yezidis and Chaldeans.

Government
Following the overthrow of Saddam Hussein in 2003 Iraq was governed by a Coalition Provisional Authority which in turn gave way to an Interim Iraqi Government. In 2005 a new constitution and country-wide elections established a federal government which defined Iraq as a democratic, federal parliamentary republic. The main elected body is the 275 strong Council of Representatives or National Assembly which in turn elects the President

and two Vice-Presidents and the Prime Minister. The Prime Minister, who holds executive authority and is the commander-in-chief of the armed forces directs a Cabinet or Council of Ministers. A Federation Council composed of representatives from the regions and governorates will also be formed in due course. At the time of going to press there are some fifteen major political parties representing the various ethnic, religious and other groups in Iraq. The Head of State is President Jalal Talabani, the Prime Minister is Nouri Al-Malaki.

Economy

Iraq is a potentially rich country with 11% of the world's oil reserves, natural gas, plenteous other natural resources, a long history of learning and literacy and the capability to diversify its economy into industry, agriculture and tourism. However, after so many years of conflict, neglect and international sanctions, Iraq's economy and infrastructure has been devastated and although the situation is slowly improving and Iraq is now generating income from the sale of oil, the focus has still to be on a programme of economic reform and development. This encompasses the physical infrastructure such as electricity generation and distribution, water mains and sewage networks, telecommunications as well as the reform of government structures and civil society, central and local government, education and healthcare systems, and the development of the role of the media, trade unions and women's groups.

Opportunities for Business in Iraq

The UKTI website provides valuable information on the conduct of business in Iraq, laws and regulations pertinent to commerce, opportunities for business, commercial contacts and news of relevant events and conferences. As mentioned on the website, British firms are already active in a range of sectors including power, water, health, telecommunications, oil and gas, construction and education.

UK companies seeking to do business in Iraq are advised in the first instance to contact the relevant UKTI International Trade Team which is given on the website and certainly one should not contemplate visiting Iraq without taking their advice. UKTI Website: www.uktradeinvest.gov.uk and follow the links to Exporting; Countries; Iraq; Contacts and Setting up.

US companies should contact the US Department of Commerce. Details of the Iraq Investment and Reconstruction Task Force (IIRTF), which assists companies pursuing reconstruction and other business opportunities in Iraq are to be found on the website: www.export.gov/iraq.

Among the organisations involved in the provision and allocation of funds and contracts for reconstruction work in Iraq are the US Department of Defence, USAID, the World Bank and in the case of UK contributed funds, the Department for International Development (DfID). The US organisation responsible for managing existing US Government funded contracts and for issuing new contracts in Iraq under the US$18.4 billion allocated by the US Congress is the Iraq Project and Contracting Office (PCO) which is managed from the US Embassy in Baghdad. The PCO website is: www.rebuilding-iraq.net Other major fund contributions are channelled through the International Reconstruction Fund Facility for Iraq (IRFFI) and administered by the World Bank and the United Nations. UK allocated funds are channelled through DfID and a significant proportion of these funds are in turn also channelled through the IRFFI.

Finally, although there is no requirement to appoint a commercial agent in Iraq, some form of local representation is considered essential for success, particularly if the security climate precludes travel to Iraq. Such representation is sometimes handled though Jordan or Kuwait. Other useful conduits for business are the various Iraqi Chambers of Commerce or the Iraqi Federation of Industries, contact details for whom are given on the UKTI website.

Official Language
Arabic and Kurdish. English is widely used in commerce. Minorities speak Farsi, Assyrian, Armenian and Turkoman.

National Flag
Three horizontal stripes of red (top), white (middle) and black (bottom) with Allah Akbar (God is Great) in green on the central white stripe.

Personal Security
At the time of going to print travel to and around Iraq is dangerous, and likely to remain so for some time. Foreign nationals have been targeted for kidnapping and execution. The situation is very fluid. Travellers thinking of going to Iraq should first read the latest FCO travel advice on their website www.fco.gov.uk and take professional advice about their personal security before making any decision about whether or not to travel there.

Visas
Information on visa regulations may be found on the Iraqi Ministry of Foreign Affairs website: www.iraqmofa.net.

Local Time GMT + 3 hours

Dialling-in Code 964

Working Hours (local time)
Government Offices: 0800-1400 Saturday to Thursday (closing time on Thursday 1300)
Banks: 0800-1400 Saturday to Thursday (closing time on Thursday 1300)
Private companies: As for government offices.
British Embassy Baghdad: 0800-1600 Sunday to Thursday
Consular Section British Embassy, Baghdad
1000-1200 Sunday to Thursday

Public Holidays
All Muslim festivals (see Chapter1).

Taxation
Companies with permanent establishments in Iraq are subject to income tax.

Currency
Iraqi Dinar (IQD). At the time of going to print the exchange rate was IQD 1,846 = £1 sterling and 1,136 = US$ 1. However, the current essential daily trading currency is the US $ in cash. The banking system is under reconstruction and there are as yet no ATM machines.

Electricity
220 volts AC 50 cycles. All types of 2 and 3 pin plugs. Light fittings bayonet and screw.

Embassies
Embassy of the Republic of Iraq in UK
9 Holland Villas Road, London W14 8BP
Tel: 020 7602 8456 or 0778 522 7703
Consulate of the Republic of Iraq in UK
169 Knightsbridge, London SW7 5QH
Tel: 020 7590 9220
Embassy of the Republic of Iraq in Washington US
3421 Massachusetts Ave, NW Washington DC 20007
Tel: (1) 202 742-1600 Ext 136
Consulate of the Republic of Iraq in Washington
1801 P Street, MW Washington DC 20036
Tel: (1) 202 483-7500
British Embassy in The Republic of Iraq
International Zone, Baghdad
Tel: + 964 (0) 7901 911 684/+ 964 (0) 7901 926 280
www.britishembBaghdad@fco.gov.uk
Consular Section of the British Embassy,
In Ocean Cliffs (opposite the al-Rasheed Hotel, behind the Convention Centre, Baghdad
All enquiries from the public should be referred to the British Embassy Baghdad.
Iraqna mobile (for emergencies involving British nationals only) (964) (0) 7901 935 149
Email: britishconsulbaghdad@yahoo.co.uk

Office of The British Embassy in Basra, Basra Air Station, Basra, Iraq. Tel: (964) 831000
Office of the British Embassy in Erbil
Communications c/o Iraq policy Unit, Foreign and commonwealth Office, King Charles street, London SW1A 2AH
US Embassy in the Republic of Iraq
APO AE 09316, Baghdad, Iraq
Tel: (1) 703 343 7604, 8202, 8204, 8205, 8207
US Consular Section
C-135, The Chancery   Tel: (1) 240 553 0584 Ext. 4354
US Embassy website: baghdad.usembassy.gov.

Further Information
FCO Country Profile and Travel Advice: www.fco.gov.uk
UK Trade & Investment Country Profile: www.uktradeinvest.gov.uk
British Embassy in Iraq
Website: www.http://ukiraq.fco.gov.uk
DfID (information and procurement procedures)
Website: www.dfid.gov.uk
Lonely Planet: *Middle East Travel Guide* – May 2010, ISBN 9781 7410 46922

I
R
A
Q

The State of Kuwait

Geography
Kuwait is situated at the head of the Arab Gulf and
borders Iraq in the north and west and Saudi Arabia
in the south. Roughly the size of Wales, it has an area
of 17,818 sq kms of mainly dry and flat, or gently
undulating gravelly desert. It has a 224 km-long
coastline with Kuwait Bay in the centre. The islands of
Bubiyan and Failaka lie off the north-east shore. At their
closest points the Kuwaiti and Iranian frontiers are only
some 15 kms apart. Al-Mutla Ridge runs along the
northwest side of Kuwait Bay and Kuwait City, the
capital and commercial centre, is located on the southern
shore. Major towns are Ahmadi, centre of the oil industry,
Fahaheel and the historical town of Jahra (Al-Jahra).
Industrial areas are located at Shuaiba and Mina
Abdullah on the southern coastline and at Shuwaikh
near Kuwait City. Shuwaikh includes the port.

Climate
The temperature during the winter months (November
to March) is generally pleasant but can be very cold at
night. Daytime temperatures vary between 14 and 24° C.
Rainfall, usually falling in winter, averages 100 mm to 370
mm. In summer, (June to September) it is very hot and
humid although not as much as Bahrain or Abu Dhabi.
Temperatures average 36°C by day. Sandstorms which
occur throughout the year, are common in early summer.

History
The origins of 'Al-Kuwait' or 'little fort' in Arabic, go back
to a settlement some three hundred years ago but the
island of Failaka is known to have been inhabited during

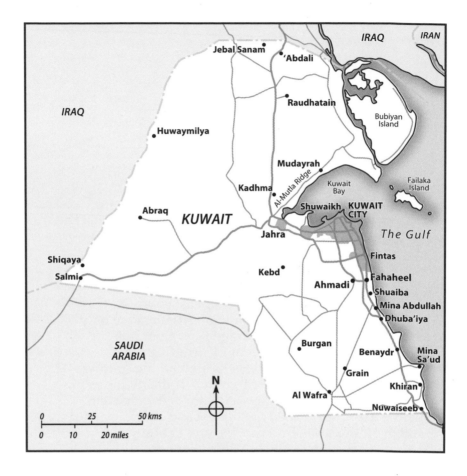

in 2nd century BC. Its importance grew, slowly at first, based on trade and pearling until in recent history it has become an immensely rich oil producing state, accounting for 3% of the world's production and 9.3% of total world reserves. A long period of protective treaty relations with Britain came to an end in 1961 when Kuwait became a fully independent state. In 1990 Kuwait was invaded and occupied by Iraq until being liberated by an international coalition in 1991. Since that time, Kuwait has had to recover from the economic, environmental and psychological damage caused by this invasion and occupation. In 1993 it was the launchpad for the invasion of Iraq.

Government
The Head of State, the Amir, His Highness Shaikh Sabah Al-Ahmad Al-Jaber Al-Sabah is a constitutional ruler of the Al-Sabah family who have ruled in the region since 1756. The Amir rules through the Prime Minister, the Crown Prince and an appointed cabinet. An elected National Assembly makes a critical examination of Government. Although political parties are illegal there are a number of informal political groupings.

Economy
Kuwait is a very wealthy country with a high per capita income and 90% of export revenue derives from oil production and the petrochemical industry. It has 10% of the world's oil reserves. Its foreign reserves and investment income are substantial. It has recovered well from the huge losses caused by the Iraqi invasion and seeks to diversify its economy. Kuwait actively promotes itself as a base for foreign investors in Iraq, although with limited success to date. Kuwait is a generous foreign aid donor. Almost all trade is conducted through Kuwaiti nationals and Kuwaiti companies. There is an active British Business Forum.

Population
2.6 million (est) Kuwaitis comprise about 50% of the population the rest being other Arabs, other nationalities

including Westerners and Asians. Annual growth rate for Kuwaiti Nationals is about 2.7%. More than half the population live in Kuwait City and its environs, in Ahmadi (264,000) and Jahra (224,000).

Religion
The state religion is Islam. Almost all Kuwaitis are Muslims. The majority are Sunni Muslims but there is a sizeable Shia minority. There are small communities of other religions and a number of churches cater for expatriates. Although the practice of other religions is restricted, there are a number of churches in Kuwait.

Official Language
Arabic. English is widely spoken in business and diplomatic circles and by expatriates working in the service sector. Farsi (Persian) is also widely understood.

National Flag
A horizontal rectangle divided into three horizontal stripes of green, white and red (top to bottom). The side on the hoist forms the base of a black trapezoid set into the stripes.

Visas
UK and US nationals can acquire a one-month visit/business visa on arrival at Kuwait International Airport for a fee. Visa regulations are explained in detail on the Kuwait Government website: www.kuwaitiah.net/ministry.html
Exchange facilities are available at the airport 24 hours a day. Otherwise a visa may be obtained in the normal way (see below) by applying to a Kuwaiti embassy abroad. Visa regulations change from time to time and it is advisable to check well in advance if possible. Passports must not contain evidence of a visit to Israel and visitors who have should seek advice from their nearest passport issuing office. There is a KD 2 airport departure tax.

Alcohol and Banned Substances
The importation of alcohol is forbidden. The prohibition of alcoholic beverages in Kuwait is strictly enforced. The use of or dealing in drugs carries severe penalties: prison sentences and fines and possibly the death penalty.

Local Time GMT + 3 hours, EST + 8 hours

Dialling Code 965

Public Holidays
All Muslim Festivals (*see* Chapter 1); New Year's Day – 1 January and National Day – 25 February.

Working Hours (local time)
Normal working week is Saturday to Wednesday and half-day on Thursday. Business hours are from 0830-1230 and 1630-2000 in winter. Some offices work only from 0700-1400 in summer.
Government offices: 0730-1330 Saturday to Wednesday in winter, and 0700-1300 Saturday to Wednesday in summer.
Oil companies: 0800-1500 Sunday to Thursday.
Banks: 0800-1200 Sunday to Thursday and some branches open in the afternoons.
British Embassy: 0730-1430 Sunday to Thursday.
The working week and working hours are sometimes extensively amended during the holy month of Ramadan.

Currency
Kuwait Dinar (KD or KWD) divided into 1,000 Fils. At the time of going to print, the exchange rate was KD 0.465 = £1 sterling and KD 0.285 = $1 US. Credit cards are widely accepted and ATMs are available in leading banks.

Income Tax
There is no personal taxation.

Electricity Supply
240 volts AC. Plugs flat-pin British type.

Transportation

The taxi fare from the airport is KD 5. There are standard fares in Kuwait City. A number of highly efficient taxi companies can also arrange a luxury limousine to pick you up from anywhere in the city within minutes of calling. Agree the price before your journey. The Kuwait National Transportation Company runs a network of modern buses along a number of routes around Kuwait City. It is permitted to drive on an International Driving Licence/Permit but if one is legally resident then a Kuwait Driving Licence is required. The national airline is Kuwait Air.

Tipping

Tips are expected by airport and hotel porters but not by taxis. Hotels and restaurants normally add a service charge.

Tourist Sites

Places of interest include Kuwait Towers, the City's main landmark on the coast road which has an observational deck, coffee shop and restaurant; Tareq Rajab Museum; the National Museum; the Old City gates; the former British Political Agency building – Dickson House Cultural Centre; the Exhibition of Kuwaiti Sailing Ships; Kuwait Scientific Centre; the Martyr's House in Qurain (where Kuwaiti resistance fighters were surrounded and attacked by Iraqi forces during the occupation in 1990-91); Kuwait House for National Works (museum of invasion and liberation).

Embassies

Embassy of the State of Kuwait in UK
2 Albert Gate, Knightsbridge, London SW1X 7JU.
Tel: 020 7590 3400; Fax: 020 7823 1712.
Embassy of the State of Kuwait in US
2940 Tilden St NW, Washington DC 20008
Tel: 202 966 0702
British Embassy in Kuwait
Arabian Gulf Street, Dasman, PO Box 2, SAFAT 13001, State of Kuwait. Tel: (+ 965) 2259 4320
Website: http://ukinkuwait.fco.gov.uk

US Embassy in Kuwait
PO Box 77 Safat 13001 Kuwait
Tel: (+ 965) 2259 1001 Fax: (+ 965) 2538 0282
Email: paskuwaitm@state.gov
Consular Section Email: consularkuwaitm@state.gov

General Comments

In spite of extensive mine clearing operations following the Gulf War there are still unexploded mines and other weapons in some areas, even those marked as 'cleared'. Mines can still be washed ashore on the beaches or uncovered in the desert. When travelling outside Kuwait City and on the offshore islands it is strongly advisable to stick to paved roads and certainly not to handle any suspect object.

Further Information

FCO Country Profile and Travel Advice: www.fco.gov.uk
UK Trade & Investment Country Profile: www.uktradeinvest.gov.uk
Lonely Planet *Middle East Tourist Guide* May 2010 ISBN 9781741046922

K
U
W
A
I
T

OMAN

The Sultanate of Oman

Geography

Oman occupies the southeastern corner of the Arabian
Peninsula. Its diverse territory covers about 309,500 sq kms
and has a 1,700 km-long coastline. Oman also includes the
isolated Musandam Peninsula overlooking the Strait of
Hormuz which is separated from the rest of the Sultanate
by UAE territory. Another small enclave, Madha, lies
within the UAE. There are a number of islands, the largest
of which is Masirah. The northern coastal strip, on the Gulf
of Oman, consists of a sand and gravelly plain known as
the Batinah Coast. Beyond this to the southwest lie the
Hajar Mountains with the highest peak being the Jebel
Akhdar (9,957 feet). This name, meaning 'Green Mountain',
is also used to refer to the complete Hajar range. Further to
the southwest, Oman borders Saudi Arabia on the edge of
the vast desert of the Rub'Al-Khali or 'Empty Quarter'.
The remainder of Oman's territory includes two large
areas of salt flats in the central region, a long southeastern
coastline on the Arabian Sea and the fertile Dhofar region
and mountain range in the south where Oman borders
the Republic of Yemen. The interior and coastline of Oman
are very beautiful. The Government implements an active
programme to protect and enhance the environment. The
capital, commercial centre and main port of Muscat is
situated on a rugged part of the north-east coast. It
comprises the districts of Muscat, Ruwi and Muttrah,
formerly referred to as the 'three cities' and now known
as 'the Capital Area'. Other major towns are Sur (south of
Muscat), Nizwa in the interior, and Salalah in the south.

Climate

Like its geography, the climate in Oman is varied. In winter,
from October to March, Muscat and the coastal region is

pleasantly warm with temperatures between 16 and 32°C. In Salalah however, it is humid with temperatures at the top end of this scale. In the summer months from April to September the coast is hot and very humid, reaching 47°C with 85% humidity between May and July. The interior is generally hot and dry except at altitude. Rainfall is very low except in Salalah and Dhofar where light monsoon rains fall from June to September.

History

The earliest settlements in Oman can be traced to the 3rd millennium BC and it was also known to have been an important independent copper-producing state. Following a period under Persian rule it achieved further importance as the main source in the world of frankincense. Converting to Islam at an early stage, the area came under the influence of the Portuguese. However, the Portuguese were evicted in 1650 and for two centuries Oman itself became an imperial power in the region. In 1646 and again in 1798, Oman entered into long-standing and friendly treaty relations with Britain and these continue to this day. Since becoming Head of State in 1970, the present ruler, His Majesty Sultan Qaboos Bin Said Al Said has used the country's oil resources to develop Oman's infrastructure, creating a modern state while at the same time preserving Oman's unique character and heritage.

Government

Oman is an absolute monarchy and His Majesty Sultan Qaboos rules through a Cabinet of Ministers. The Sultan is a member of the Al Bu Said dynasty who have governed in the region since 1749. There is also a Consultative Council, the *Majlis Ash-Shura*, which is elected by universal adult suffrage and a State Council (*Majlis Al-Dowla*) of appointed Ministers. The Sultan maintains a personal style of government, touring the country for several weeks each spring to meet his people. The Government follows an active Omanisation programme
to replace expatriates with Omanis and this has had a large measure of success.

Economy
Oman's economy is is largely dependent on the production of oil and gas which provides by far the largest part of the country's export revenues although production in terms of the other Gulf producers is relatively modest. Since production began in 1967 oil revenues have been used to establish an efficient infrastructure including a road network, housing and electricity. A priority has also been placed on defence. In 1975 the Government defeated an eleven-year-long armed revolt in the southern region of Dafur. Oman is successfully diversifying its economy by exploiting gas, copper and other mineral deposits, expanding the agricultural, fishing and tourism industries, and industrial development. Another important economic policy is 'Omanisation', the replacement of migrant workers with Omani nationals to provide work for the growing number of young Omanis.

Population
The Omani population of roughly 3.3 million (Juy 2007) is predominately Arab but includes Baluchi, Lawati and Gujarati communities and 577,000 expatriates, mainly from South Asia. Most of the population live in Muscat and the Batinah Coastal Plain. The growth rate of Omani nationals is around 3.6% per annum.

Religion
The State religion is Islam. Most Omanis are Ibadhi Muslims. There is an influential Shia Muslim community in the capital area, and some Sunnis, mainly in the south. Non-Muslim religious observance is tolerated and there are Christian churches and Hindu temples both in the Capital Area and in Salalah.

Official Language
Arabic, but English is widely spoken. Swahili, Farsi, Urdu, Baluchi and a number of Indian languages are also commonly spoken.

**O
M
A
N**

OMAN

National Flag

A vertical red band on the hoist within the top of which is superimposed a white *khanjar* (or *khanja*) (the traditional dagger of the region) and crossed swords. To the right of the red band are three horizontal bands of white (top), red and green (bottom).

Visas

British passport holders can obtain an entry visa on arrival at any land, sea or air entry port in Oman: either

- A one-month combined tourist/business visa costing OMR 6. This can be extended for one month for a further OMR 6.
- A one-year multiple entry visa, which is valid for three weeks per visit, after which you must leave Oman for at least three weeks before returning (though this condition is under review).

Overstaying without proper authority can lead to fines of OMR 10 per day. Travellers holding other than British passports should check with an Omani Embassy or Consulate on the rules applicable to them. Since Omani visa rules are under review as part of the Omani effort to encourage tourism, it is wise for all travellers to check on the latest situation either at an Omani Embassy or on a reliable website such as www.omanembassy.org.uk or the FCO website: www.fco.gov.uk.

Alcohol and Prohibited Substances

Alcoholic drinks are sold in certain hotels and restaurants. Non-Muslim visitors arriving by air are permitted to import two bottle of alcoholic beverage. This is not, however, permitted when entering by road. Non-Muslim residents may apply for an alcohol allowance.

The import and use of narcotics and obscene material is forbidden and can lead to imprisonment. There are severe penalties for drugs offences including, in some cases, the death penalty.

Local Time GMT + 4 hours, EST + 9 hours.

Dialling Code 968

Working Hours (local time)
Business: 0800-1300 and 1530-1830 Saturday to Thursday.
Government offices: 0730-1430 Saturday to Wednesday.
Banks: 1800-1200 Saturday to Wednesday and 0800-1130 Thursday.
Shops: 0800-1300 and 1600-1800 Saturday to Wednesday and 0800-1300 Thursday.
British Embassy office hours: 0730-1430 Saturday to Wednesday. The working week and working hours are sometimes extensively amended during the holy month of Ramadan.

Public Holidays
Most Muslim festivals (*see* Chapter 1); National Day and the Birthday of HM The Sultan – both on 18 November.

Taxation
There is a double taxation agreement between Oman and UK, but personal income is not taxed in Oman.

Currency
Omani Riyal (OMR) divided into 1,000 Baizas. At the time of going to print, the exchange rate was OMR 0.624 = £1 sterling. It is tied to the US$ at US$1 = OMR 0.384. Major credit cards are accepted and cash is available at ATMs through Cirrus and other international networks.

Electricity
220/240 volts. Plugs either 2-pin or 3-pin flat British type.

Transportation
The Capital Area's airport is Seeb International Airport, 40 kms west of Muscat. It is well served by several major airlines including BA, Emirates and Gulf Air (jointly owned by Oman, Bahrain and Abu Dhabi

O
M
A
N

(UAE). The national carrier is Oman Air which services domestic airports and some other regional and subcontinental destinations. There are some international flights to Salalah. The National Bus Company runs inter-city routes, and a service to Dubai. The taxi service is good, although few taxis have meters or fixed fares. The fare to Muscat from Seeb International Airport is around OMR 8.

Tourist Sites

Although Oman is now actively encouraging tourism, there are as yet no tourist offices but a number of tour companies and the larger hotels offer tours. There are an almost overwhelming number of sites of interest in Muscat, Nizwa, Salalah and the mountains, oases and farms in the interior with their *falaj* or irrigation channels. Sea and coastal trips, diving, visits to the principal museums, the *souqs,* the forts and other national buildings make Oman one of the most interesting tourist locations in the region.

Tipping

Taxis are not tipped. In restaurants, if there is 10% service charge, tipping is not necessary. A Government tax of 17% is added to all hotel bills.

Embassies

Embassy of the Sultanate of Oman in UK
167 Queens Gate, London SW7 5HE
Tel: 020 7225 0001; Fax 020 7589 2505
Embassy of the Sultanate of Oman in US
2535 Belmont Road NW, Washington DC 200008
Tel: 202 387 1980; Fax: 202 745 4933
British Embassy in Muscat
PO Box 185, Mina AL-Fahal, Post Code 116, Sultanate of Oman.
Tel: (+ 968) 24 609000; Fax: (+ 968) 24 609010
Website: http://ukinoman.fco.gov.uk/en
US Embassy in Muscat

Jameat A'Duwal Al-Arabiya Street, Shatti al-Qurm
Diplomatic Area. Tel: (+968) 24 698989
Website: http:/oman.usembassy.gov

General Comments
Oman has many features of an open and liberal society
and the Omanis in the Capital Area are cosmopolitan
by Gulf Arab standards. The underlying culture is
nevertheless conservative, particularly in rural areas
which have only been open to foreigners in the last 20-25
years. For this reason visitors should dress soberly,
particularly in public places. As in all Gulf countries
care should be exercised with photography. Omanis are
sensitive about security; always obtain permission to take
photographs of all but obvious tourist sites. Finally, as
elsewhere, do not photograph women.

Further Information
FCO Country Profile and Travel Advice: www.fco.gov.uk
UK Trade & Investment Country Profile:
www.uktradeinvest.gov.uk
Lonely Planet *Oman, UAE & Arabian Peninsular Travel
Guide* September 2007 ISBN: 9781741045468

O
M
A
N

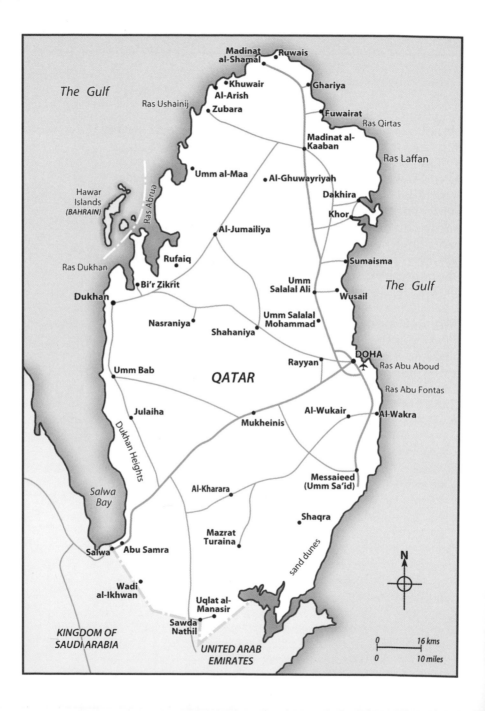

QATAR

The Gulf

Madinat al-Shamal ● Ruwais

● Khuwair
Al-Arish
Ras Ushainij ● Zubara
● Ghariya

● Fuwairat
Ras Qirtas

Madinat al-Kaaban

Ras Laffan

● Umm al-Maa ● Al-Ghuwayriyah

Hawar Islands (BAHRAIN)

Ras Abrua

Dakhira

Khor

● Al-Jumailiya

Ras Dukhan

● Rufaiq
● Sumaisma

● Bi'r Zikrit

Umm Salalal Ali
Wusail

Dukhan

The Gulf

Nasraniya ●
Shahaniya ●
Umm Salalal Mohammad

Umm Bab ●

QATAR

Rayyan ●

DOHA
Ras Abu Aboud

Ras Abu Fontas

● Julaiha

Al-Wukair
● Al-Wakra

Mukheinis ●

Dukhan Heights

Salwa Bay

Al-Kharara ●

Messaieed (Umm Sa'id)

● Shaqra

sand dunes

Salwa ● Abu Samra

Mazrat Turaina

Wadi al-Ikhwan ●

Uqlat al-Manasir

Sawda Nathil

KINGDOM OF SAUDI ARABIA

UNITED ARAB EMIRATES

N

0 ———— 16 kms
0 ———— 10 miles

The State of Qatar

Geography

The Qatar Peninsula lies midway down the southern shore of the Arabian Gulf just southeast of Bahrain. The country is about 170 kms long and 90 kms wide at its widest point with a total area of 11,437 sq kms. The territory is mainly flat gravelly desert except for some low hills in the north-west and sand dunes with some marshes in the south where it borders Saudi Arabia. The capital city and commercial centre, Doha (Ad-Dawha), situated on the East coast, is a thriving modern city. It is also the location of the international airport and one of Qatar's ports. Major towns are Umm Said, south of Doha and the centre of Qatar's petrochemical industry, also with a port, and Dukhan on the west coast, the centre for the country's onshore oil production. Ras Laffan Industrial City, north of Doha is being developed as the centre for production of Qatar's liquefied natural gas.

Climate

Pleasant from November to April but hot and humid from May to October. From July to September temperatures can rise to 44°C with humidity over 85%. Sandstorms occur throughout the year especially in spring.

History

Qatar's (pronounced *Gatter*) history is associated with the Al-Thani family since the country became established in the 18th century as a traditional centre for pearling. The first Emir (or Amir), Shaikh Mohammed bin Thani, came to power in the mid 19th century and Doha became the country's capital city. Qatar subsequently entered into a number of treaty relations first with the Turks and later in 1916 with the British until declaring independence in

1971 when the British left the region. Oil was discovered in 1939 but because of the Second World War was not commercially exploited until 1949.

Government
Qatar is an absolute monarchy. The Amir, His Highness Shaikh Hamad bin Khalifa Al-Thani, rules with the assistance of an appointed Advisory Council which discusses legislation prior to promulgation. The Amir is committed to a programme of political reform aimed at increasing popular participation in decision making, modernisation, openness and media freedom. A new constitution has been introduced, paving the way for elections to a Legislative Council.

Economy
Qatar's economy is predominantly based on oil although its reserves are small in comparison with its neighbours. Its natural gas resources on the other hand, in the initial stages of exploitation, are among the world's largest. Gas constitutes Qatar's priority for economic development although it is also the Government's policy to diversify the economy where possible and this has met with some measure of success particularly in the petrochemical field.

In addition to the Commercial Section at the British Embassy, the British businessman can look for advice from the Qatar British Business Forum.
Website: ww.qbbf.com

Miscellaneous Information
The national airline is Qatar Airways. The Qatar Government owns Al-Jazeera, the satellite TV station which broadcasts in English and Arabic and has an estimated audience of 130 million people.

Population
The population is estimated to be approximately 1.4 million of which some 400,000 are Qatari nationals. The remainder are foreign expatriate workers from Europe, the Indian sub-continent, Asia and other countries.

Religion
The state religion is Islam.

Official Language
Arabic, but English is widely used.

National Flag
This is divided by a vertical serrated band which is one third white on the hoist side and two thirds dark purple on the right side.

Local Time GMT + 3 hours, EST + 8 hours

Dialling Code 974

Visas
British citizens and nationals from a number of other Western countries can obtain a single, short stay (21 days) tourist or business visa on arrival at Doha airport or other points of entry. The cost is QAR 55. This can be extended in-country for a further 14 days. Again, the cost is QAR 55. Longer-term or multi-entry visas are obtained in the normal way by application to a Qatari embassy abroad (*See* Embassies below). Since visa regulations cover numerous options and are continually being updated, it is advisable to check current regulations well in advance. There is an airport departure tax of QAR 20.

Alcohol and Prohibited Substances
The importation of alcohol, narcotics, pornography, pork products and religious books and material is strictly forbidden. Penalties for the possession of or trading in drugs are particularly severe and often result in prison sentences. However, alcohol is available to non-Muslims in licensed hotel restaurants and bars but only to guests or those who have purchased membership. Non-Muslim expatriates can obtain alcohol on a permit system but must follow local regulations for transportation and consumption. Finally, it is an offence to drink alcohol in

a public place or to be drunk in public. Penalties include prison sentences and deportation.

Public Holidays
The main Muslim festivals (*see* Chapter 1); National Day – 3 September.

Working Hours (local time)
Government offices: Saturday to Thursday 0700-1300.
Businesses: Saturday to Thursday 0800-1200 and1600-1900, half day on Thursday.
Oil companies: Sunday to Thursday 0700-1500
Banks: Sunday to Thursday 0730-1300
British Embassy: Sunday to Thursday 0730-1430.
The working week and working hours are sometimes extensively amended during the holy month of Ramadan.

Currency
Qatar Riyal (QAR) divided into 100 Dirhams, also commonly called Halalas. At the time of going to print, the exchange rate was QAR 5.914 = £1 sterling. The Qatar Riyal is tied to US $ at QAR 3.639 = US$1.

Electricity
220/240 volts AC. Light fittings – bayonet and screw. Plugs 3 pin flat most common.

Transportation
Large hotels have a pick up service from the airport. Taxis have a fixed hourly hire rate. Driving is permitted on a UK licence for up to 7 days, after which a local licence must be purchased and is valid for 3 months. Cost QAR50. Drivers must be over 21 years of age.

Tipping
No tip if service charge (normally 15%) is added. Airport porters, 100 fils per item of baggage. Taxi drivers and others, around 5% is customary.

Embassies
Embassy of the State of Qatar in UK
1 South Audley Street, London W1Y 1NB
Tel: 020 7493 2200; Fax 020 7493 2661
Embassy of the State of Qatar in US
4200 Wisconsin Avenue, NW Suite 200, Washington DC
20016; tel: 202 274 1603
British Embassy in Doha
PO Box 3 Doha, Qatar
Tel: (+ 974) 496 2000
Website: http://ukinqatar.fco.gov.uk
US Embassy in Doha
22nd February Street, Al-Luqta District, PO Box 2399
Website: http://qatar.usembassy.gov

Tourist Sites
Tour companies offer tours, mainly for groups, to sites
of interest such as the National and Ethnographic and
Postal Museums, Doha Fort, The Old Police Station,
Zoo and Camel Racing.

Further Information
FCO Country Profile and Travel Advice: www.fco.gov.uk
UK Trade & Investment Country Profile:
www.uktradeinvest.gov.uk
Lonely Planet *Middle East Tourist Guide* May 2010
ISBN: 9781741046922
Gorilla Guides, *London: The Business Travellers' Guide to
Qatar*, ISBN 1903185 068

Q
A
T
A
R

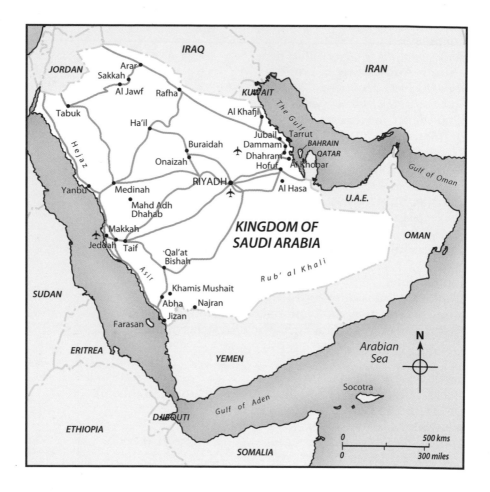

The Kingdom of Saudi Arabia

Geography

Saudi Arabia occupies most of the Arabian Peninsula with an area of about 2.25 million sq kms. It consists largely of desert but there are also extensive mountainous areas. The Hejaz and Asir regions in the west and southwest respectively contain continuous mountain ranges of the same names running the length of the Red Sea coast. The Asir mountain region with its forests is particularly striking. These mountain ranges give way in the central region (Nejd) to the deserts of the large central plateau. Finally, the Eastern Province (Al-Hasa) is bounded by the Arabian Gulf. It takes its name from the extensive Al-Hasa oasis but otherwise consists of low lying desert with some salt flats (*sabkha*). In the north of the country lies the huge Nafud desert and in the southeast the vast desert of the 'Empty Quarter' (*Rub'Al-Khali*). Called 'The Sands' by the Bedu, it is the largest sand desert in the world. The Kingdom contains the two holiest cities of Islam, Makkah (*Makkah Al-Mukarama*) and Madinah (*Al-Madina Al-Munawwara*). Riyadh is the capital city, seat of Government and an increasingly important commercial centre. Jeddah, on the Red Sea coast is the principal port and main centre for private sector business. Yanbu, north of Jeddah, is a major industrial city. The other large industrial and commercial concentration and centre for the oil, gas and petrochemical industry is in the Eastern Province, based on the towns of Dammam (the country's second major port), Al-Khobar and Dhahran.

Climate

Riyadh has a typically desert climate, very hot but dry in summer, with extremes of temperature between day and night. From April to September temperatures rise to 45°C but from December to February it is pleasant with temperatures below 20°C by day and even lower by night. Jeddah and the towns of the eastern region are hot in summer with temperatures averaging 30°C. Humidity rises to 90% particularly in September. In winter it is cooler with temperatures as in Riyadh of below 20°C. Rain storms occur in winter and spring, particularly in the coastal regions and there are occasional dust storms.

History

The history of Saudi Arabia embodies the history of the whole Peninsula. The earliest settlements in the 4th and 5th millennium BC, the Nabataean civilisation, the Arab and Bedu heritage, the home of the Arabic language and the birthplace of Islam, the rise of the House of Saud, the discovery of vast oil resources and finally, the establishment of the modern state. The magnificent remains of part of the Nabataean civilisation can be seen at Madain Salih in the northwest of Saudi Arabia. The First Saudi State was established in 1747 when Mohammed Ibn Saud formed a lasting family alliance with the great Islamic reformer Mohammed Ibn Abdul Al-Wahab, the followers of whom still predominate in Saudi Arabia today. The capital at that time was Dir'iyyah, (just outside Riyadh). The modern Kingdom of Saudi Arabia was founded in 1932 by one of the region's most remarkable leaders, Abdul Aziz bin Abdul Rahman Al-Saud. After a lengthy and difficult struggle, King Abdul Aziz, or Ibn Saud as he is often called, finally succeeded in capturing the cities and unifying the tribes of this vast region and establishing The Kingdom of Saudi Arabia. Although oil was discovered in the Kingdom in 1938, it was not fully exploited until the 1950s (because of the Second World War). King Abdul Aziz was succeeded in power by his sons who have presided over the development of the modern state in existence today.

Government

The Head of State and Supreme Religious Leader is King Abdullah bin Abdul Aziz Al Saud. He is officially entitled 'The Custodian of the Two Holy Mosques' (and not 'His Majesty'). The Kingdom of Saudi Arabia is a monarchy but with a political system rooted in Islamic Sharia law. The King rules through a Council of Ministers and a Consultative Council (*Majlis Al-Shura*) and there is also widespread consultation with the Royal family, the religious establishment and the business community.

Economy

By far the largest and most wealthy country of the region, Saudi Arabia dominates the politics and the economy of the Peninsula. It is the world's leading oil exporter with more than 25% of the world's proven oil reserves and the highest GNP in the Arab world. Although the economy is dominated by oil, strenuous efforts have been made to diversify into other fields. It now has one of the world's largest petrochemical industries. Ambitious projects have emphasised industrial and urban development, defence and education as well as agriculture, mining and water development. The construction industry, although it has slowed in the last decade, nevertheless thrives. The Government is committed to privatisation starting with the telecommunication and power generation sectors and encourages joint-ventures in many areas of economic activity. The Government has also instituted an active policy of 'Saudisation' (replacing foreign workers with Saudi nationals).

Saudi Arabia is an active export market for a large range of Western products. Although not obliged to appoint an agent in Saudi Arabia, most companies wishing to enter the market do so. In addition to contact with the Commercial Section of the British Embassy there are active British Business Groups in Riyadh, Jeddah and the Eastern Province. Contact details are given on the UK Trade and Investment website: www.uktradeinvest.gov.uk.

Population
The total population is estimated at 27.6 million (2007 estimate), of whom 7 million are expatriate workers from other Arab countries, the Indian sub-continent, Africa, Asia, Europe and USA. Over 50% of the rapidly increasing Saudi population are under 20 years of age.

Religion
The State religion is Islam and the Saudi population is 100 per cent Muslim of whom 90% are Sunni and 10% are Shia. The practice of other religions is forbidden.

Official Language
Arabic, although English is widely spoken in business and official circles and by expatriates working in the service sector. All official correspondence with Government establishments must be in Arabic (and normally English as well) and carry the Hejirian date as well as the Gregorian.

National Flag and Official Emblem
Light green bearing the Muslim creed 'There is no god but God, (and) Muhammad is His Prophet', below which is a horizontal traditional sword. The official Saudi Arabian emblem is a date palm representing vitality and growth under which are two crossed swords symbolising justice and strength rooted in faith.

Local Time GMT + 3 hours. EST + 8 hours.

Dialling Code
966-1 (Riyadh), 966-2 (Jeddah) 966-3 (Dhahran).

Public Holidays
The only festivals celebrated are the *Eid Al-Adha* and *Eid Al-Fitr* when extended holiday breaks are taken (*see* Chapter 1 for dates).

Visas
All visitors to Saudi Arabia, including pilgrims, require visas. Application is made to a Saudi Embassy abroad

and must be accompanied by a letter of invitation from a Saudi sponsor. The expiry date of the passport must extend for six months beyond the date of the visit. The passport should not contain evidence of a visit to Israel or an Israeli place of birth or entry may be refused. Women travelling alone must be met by their sponsors or their entry to the Kingdom may be delayed. British residents in Saudi Arabia require a valid exit/re-entry permit from the Saudi Ministry of Interior in order to leave the country. There is no airport departure tax. Visa regulations change from time to time and it is always advisable to check well in advance from a reputable website such as the Saudi Embassy in London www.saudiembassy.org.uk – 'travel' and 'visas'

Alcohol and Prohihited Goods
The importation, possession and consumption of alcohol is strictly forbidden and can incur heavy penalties including imprisonment, corporal punishment and deportation. A person arriving in the Kingdom in an inebriated state is liable to arrest and deportation. The importation of goods with an alcoholic content, pork products, pornography, magazines which depict partly clad people, particularly women, religious books (other than the Holy Quran) and literature and artifacts are also strictly prohibited. Magazines which depict women are likely to be confiscated or censored. Video tapes, and sometimes floppy discs and CD Roms, are likely to be inspected by customs officials before they may be imported. Finally, drug smuggling is a capital offence in Saudi Arabia and this warning is printed on every immigration form. Medications should be clearly labelled in their original containers and a doctor's prescription for the medicine should also be carried.

Working Hours
Government offices: 0730-1430 Saturday to Wednesday.
Business: Riyadh 0800-1300 and 1600-2000 Saturday to Wednesday and 0800-1300 Thursday; Jeddah 0900-1300 and 1600-2000 Saturday to Wednesday and 0900-1300

SAUDI ARABIA

Thursday; Eastern Province 0800-1300 and 1500-1800 Saturday to Wednesday and 0800-1300 Thursday. *Banks*: Riyadh 0830-1200 and 1630-1830 Saturday to Wednesday and 0830-1200 Thursday; Jeddah 0830-1200 and 1700-1900 Saturday to Wednesday and 0800-1130 Thursday; Eastern Province 0800-1130 and 1600-1800 Saturday to Wednesday and 0800-1130 Thursday. In the holy month of Ramadan all Banks work from 1000-1300 Saturday to Thursday.
Shops: 0800 or 0830-1200 and 1600-2100/2200 Saturday to Thursday. Shops and some offices close for prayers four times a day. Prayer times, which differ each day are published in advance in local newspapers.
The British Embassy in Riyadh, the British Consulate General in Jeddah and the British Trade Office in Al-Khobar: 0800-1500 Saturday to Wednesday. The working week and working hours are often extensively curtailed during Ramadan.

Currency
Saudi Riyal (SR/SAR) divided into 100 Halalah. At the time of going to print, the exchange rate was SAR 6.9 = £1 sterling. The Saudi Riyal is pegged to the $ US at US$1 = SAR 3.75. All credit cards are accepted and major banks are linked to at least one international ATM network.

Income Tax
No income tax is imposed in Saudi Arabia, although payment of *zakat* (*see* page 32) is obligatory for all practicing businesses.

Electricity Suppy
A mixture of 110 volt and 220 volt, 60 cycles with two-pin European type plugs and three-pin flat British type. Light bulbs are both bayonet and screw fitting. Industry uses 380 volt AC 60 cycles.

Transportation
Taxis are yellow and are required to carry a meter and visible registration details. Many taxis do not use the meters

and if so it is best to agree the fare in advance. Hire cars are available although for a short visit local taxis, the Saudi limousines service or a chauffeur driven car are strongly recommended. Driving can be hazardous, especially for a newcomer, and the consequences of involvement in an accident can be seriously inconvenient. Follow the advice given in Chapter 4 on *Transportation* and *Emergencies and Car Accidents*. The driving licences of Western countries are accepted when hiring a car or when applying for a Saudi driving licence, but International Driving Licences are not. Women are not allowed to drive (*see* General Comments below). It is forbidden for non-Muslims to travel within the limits of the holy cities of Makkah and Madinah. The national airline is Saudia.

Tipping
Taxis are not tipped. Tips for restaurants are usual and in the region of 10%. SR 5 to airport porters per item of baggage.

Embassies
The Royal Embassy of Saudi Arabia in UK
30 Charles Street, Mayfair, London W1J 5DZ
Tel: 020 7917 3000.
The Royal Embassy of Saudi Arabia in US
601 New Hampshire Avenue NW, Washington DC, 20037
Tel: 202 342 3800
The British Embassy in the Kingdom of Saudi Arabia (Riyadh Diplomatic Quarter): PO Box 94351, Riyadh 11693
Kingdom of Saudi Arabia Tel: 00 966 1 488 0077.
Duty Officer out of hours genuine emergency mobile numbers for Riyadh and Jeddah are given on the Embassy website: http://ukinsaudiarabia.fco.gov.uk
British Consulate General: PO Box 393, Jeddah 21411
Tel: 00966 2 622 5550; Fax 0966 2 622 6249
British Trade Office: PO Box 1868, Al-Khobar 31952
Tel: 00 966 3 882 5300; Fax: 00 966 3 882 5384
US Embassy in the Kingdom of Saudi Arabia (Riyadh Diplomatic Quarter) Website: http://riyadh.usembassy.gov
US Consulate General in Jeddah: Falasteen Street, Ruwais District. Tel: 00 966 2 667 0080.

Tourist Sites

Tourism is being developed for Saudi citizens and those of the Arab Gulf states but not as yet for other foreigners, although a few tours are arranged through UK travel agents, companies such as Bales Worldwide Travel, and some hotels in Saudi Arabia. However, for visitors and residents alike, Saudi Arabia offers a wealth of sites of interest. These include the Asir mountain region, diving in the Red Sea, the old Hejaz railway, the spectacular carved rock tombs at Madain Salah, the Masmak Fortress in Riyadh, the ruins of the old capital of Dir'iyyah and the escarpment outside Riyadh, to mention just a few. All leading hotels have information on sites of interest and bookshops stock a number of good guides. Permits are required to visit sites of historical interest which can be obtained from the Director General of the Department of Antiquities at the National Museum in Riyadh. Applications are made in person or by faxing the details of the request with copies of the main pages of your passport and visa, to Fax no: 00 966 1 411 2054. Permits take about a day to process. Foreign residents are required to produce their residence permit (*iqama*). It is forbidden for non-Muslims to travel within the limits of the holy cities of Makkah and Madinah.

General Comments

Saudi Arabia, the location of the holy cities of Makkah and Madinah, is the most conservative of all the Peninsula states and the Islamic code of behaviour and law are strictly enforced. Western men and women should dress conservatively in public, a man wearing slacks and long sleeved shirt and a woman an *abaya*, the thin black, ankle-length robe. A Western woman is certainly not required to be veiled or cover her head but it is sensible to carry a head scarf, particularly if she has long or blond hair, in case (as occasionally happens) she is told to cover it by the *Mutawwa*, the religious police. It is their job to monitor public behaviour and ensure it conforms to Islamic norms and although one does not often come into contact with them, if they give you an order, it is best to accede quickly and quietly. Always keep calm and at all costs avoid a confrontation. Women are not permitted to drive in Saudi Arabia and therefore must have a driver, and must sit in the rear seat. Strictly speaking, apart from her driver, a woman may not appear in public accompanied by a man other than her husband or close blood relative, such as her father or brother. Shops and restaurants are obliged to shut at prayer times for about 25 minutes. These times are published in the daily press. As in all Peninsula countries, exercise great care with photography. It is forbidden to photograph government buildings, palaces, military installations, airports, ports and industrial sites. Obtain permission before photographing men and do not photograph women. The majority of Western expatriates in Saudi Arabia live in private compounds which have communal amenities and where it is possible to enjoy a more Western lifestyle. The compound also affords a measure of security. Travellers to Saudi Arabia are strongly recommended to acquaint themselves with the advice on Saudi Arabian laws and customs given on the FCO website under 'Travel Advice'.

Further Information
FCO Country Profile and Travel Advice: www.fco.gov.uk
UK Trade & Investment Country Profile:
www.uktradeinvest.gov.uk
The Kingdom of Saudi Arabia, The Business Traveller's Handbook, published by Gorilla Guides ISBN: 190318503 3
Lonely Planet: *Oman, UAE & Arabian Peninsula Travel Guide* September 2007 ISBN: 9781741045468

S
A
U
D
I

A
R
A
B
I
A

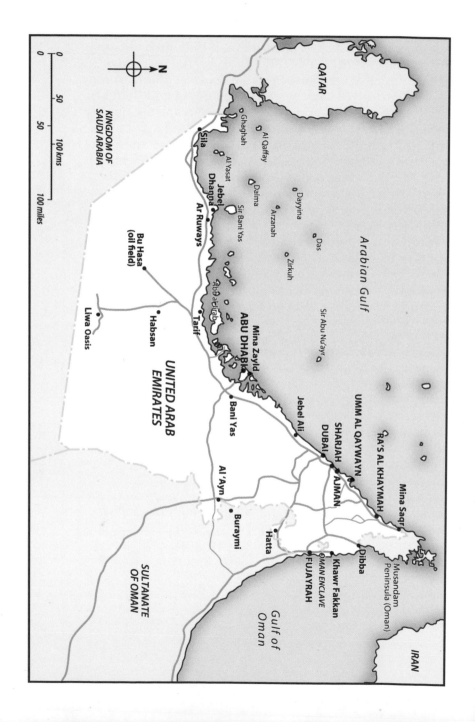

United Arab Emirates

Geography

The United Arab Emirates (UAE), lies at the lower end
of the Gulf and is a federation of seven autonomous
shaikhdoms – Abu Dhabi, Dubai, Sharjah, Fujairah, Umm
Al-Quwain, Ajman and Ras Al-Khaimah – each Emirate
being named after its principal town and the last five
being known as the Northern Emirates. The total area is
about 83,600 sq kms with some 700 kms of coastline on
the Gulf and the Gulf of Oman. Abu Dhabi is the largest
Emirate with 85% of the land area. Fujairah lies on the
Gulf of Oman. The terrain is mainly desert with salt flats
(*subkha*), along the coast and two inland oases at Buraimi
(Al-Ain) and Liwa. The Hajar Mountain range runs into
the northern part of the UAE from Oman and continues
into the Omani enclave of the Musamdam Peninsula. The
UAE also has a number of offshore islands and coral reefs.
The capital, Abu Dhabi, is a striking, modern city of
towering skyscrapers interspersed with parks, mosques
and considerable vegetation. It is the seat of the Federal
Government and the Emirate is the centre of the country's
oil, gas and petrochemical industry. The Emirate's other
large city is Al-Ain, 160 kms east of Abu Dhabi, a natural
oasis and the UAE's main agricultural centre. Dubai, the
second largest Emirate, is situated to the northeast and is
another striking modern city, the entrepôt for the region
with a vibrant tourist industry and a thriving free trade
zone at Jebel Ali. In the Northern Emirates, Sharjah is the
UAE's main manufacturing base and the remainder are
establishing an increasing number of industrial plants. Ras
Al-Khaimah is the main farming area and Fujairah, on the
Gulf of Oman, has a developing port and expanding free
trade zone.

Climate
The winter, from November to April is pleasant with temperatures between 10 and 30°C and the summers are hot with temperatures up to 45°C. Humidity is high in the coastal regions. There are occasional heavy rain falls in December and January.

History
The earliest traces of settlement in the territory date from the 3rd millennium BC. Following the Islamic conquest, the region came under Portuguese and later Persian influence. In the 18th century the Qawasim and Bani Yas tribes came to prominence and the former, a seafaring race based in Sharjah and Ras Al-Khaimah, were so active that the British named the area the Pirate Coast. The Qawasim strongly opposed the rise of British naval power in the Gulf but were eventually defeated in 1820. Britain then entered into a series of treaties, normalising shipping in the region, which became known as The Trucial Coast. The Bani Yas tribe, however, became the main power in the Bedu hinterland, based originally on the Liwa oasis but then splitting into two branches in Abu Dhabi and Dubai; the forebears of the present ruling families. The traditional occupations at that time were fishing and pearling. In 1892 Britain entered into further 'exclusive'agreements with the tribes under which they accepted formal protection and agreed not to deal with any other foreign power. In the late 19th and early 20th centuries Sharjah was the predominant Shaikhdom but Dubai then rose to prominence as a major trading centre under the Maktoum family. In recent decades, with the exploitation of immense oil reserves, Abu Dhabi has assumed prime position in the federation under the leadership of the late Shaikh Zayed Bin Sultan Al-Nahayan, while Dubai retains its position as a major trading and commercial centre. With Britain's withdrawal from the Gulf in 1971, the Shaikhdoms assumed full independence and the present federation was formed, Ras Al-Khaimah joining in 1972. The establishment of the modern state of the UAE since that time is a truly remarkable achievement by any standards.

Government

The UAE is governed by a Federal Supreme Council of
the rulers of the seven Emirates. They elect a President
who in turn appoints the Council of Ministers. The
President is Sheikh Khalifa Bin Zayed Al-Nahyan, Ruler
of Abu Dhabi, whose father, Shaikh Zayed Bin Sultan Al-
Nahayan held the Presidency from independence until
his death in 2004 . The Vice-President and Prime Minister
is Shaikh Maktoum Bin Rashid Al-Maktoum, Ruler of
Dubai. Other posts are distributed among the Emirates.
There is also a 40-member Federal National Council
appointed proportionately by the rulers of the Emirates
which acts in a consultative and advisory role to the
Supreme Council. The individual Emirates exercise
internal administrative authority.

Economy

Predominantly based on oil, but diversifying into other
fields. In addition to an expanding gas and petrochemical
industry, the UAE is also developing its free zones,
industrial and manufacturing plants and agriculture,
and undertaking major development works in electrical
power and water desalination, which increasingly involve
privatisation, PFI and BOOT projects. Abu Dhabi also
places a strong emphasis on Offset (*see* Chapter 6 –
Background Publications; Countertrade and Offset). The two
wealthiest Emirates are Abu Dhabi and Dubai. Abu Dhabi
has 9% of the world's proven oil reserves, 5% of gas
reserves and its revenue from oil and gas may now be
matched by its investments. Abu Dhabi contributes 75%
of the Federal budget and is a generous donor of overseas
development aid. Dubai, with lower oil production, has
successfully diversified its economy and is now the major
regional centre for trade. It has two ports, an aluminium
smelter, a large free zone, an established tourist industry
and property market, recently allowing foreigners to buy
property freehold. Dubai owns the airline, Emirates.
Dubai and the Northern Emirates account for 25% of
federal revenues. (*See also* Dubai and the Northern
Emirates under *Geography* above). British Business Groups

are established in Abu Dhabi and Dubai; contact details:
Abu Dhabi Tel: 00 971 2 445 7234; Fax: 00 971 2 444 0605
and Dubai Tel: 00 971 4 397 0303;
Fax: 00 971 4 397 0939.

Population
Estimated at 3.48 million, of whom approximately 80%
are expatriates (from other Arab countries, the West,
the Indian subcontinent and Asia). The population
distribution is Abu Dhabi 40%, Dubai 25% and the
remainder in the Northern Emirates.

Religion
The state religion is Islam. Ninety percent of the population
are Muslims. There are however, Christian churches and
Hindu temples in Abu Dhabi, Dubai (including Jebel Ali)
and Sharjah.

Official Language
Arabic. English is widely used in business and official
circles and by most expatriates in the service sector.
Urdu and Farsi are also widely spoken.

National Flag
A red vertical stripe along the hoist for a quarter of the
width of the flag and three horizontal stripes in the
remaining three quarters of green (top), white (middle)
and black (bottom).

Visas
GCC citizens and British citizens with the right of
abode in UK do not need a visa to visit UAE, but if
planning to stay longer than 60 days, they should
contact UAE immigration on arrival. Passports must be
valid for six months beyond the period of stay. A one
month stay is granted on entry which can be extended.
All other nationalities require a visa which is obtainable
from UAE embassies abroad. There is no airport
departure tax.

UAE

Alcohol and Prohibited Goods

Non-Muslims (arriving by air only) are permitted to import two litres of alcoholic beverage, except into Sharjah, where alcohol is banned. Alcohol is available for non-Muslims in most leading hotels (except in Sharjah) although prices are high. Non-Muslim residents can obtain a licence for a limited allocation of alcohol provided their income is above a certain level and their sponsor agrees. Public display of intoxication carries severe penalties as does driving under the influence of alcohol. The importation of narcotics, pork products and pornographic material is prohibited. Video cassettes may be censored. The penalties for drug trafficking and possession are severe and can carry the death penalty.

Local Time GMT + 4 hours, EST + 9 hours

Dialling Codes

Abu Dhabi, 00 971 2; Dubai and Jebel Ali, 00 971 4; Sharjah and Ajman, 00 971 6; Ras Al-Khaimah 00 971 7; Fujairah 00 971 9.

Public Holidays

All Muslim Festivals (*see* Chapter 1), and Christian Holidays (Easter and Christmas); New Year's Day, Ruler's Accession Day 6th August, (Abu Dhabi only) and National Day 2nd and 3rd December.

Working Hours

Government offices: 0730-1330 Sunday to Thursday in winter and 0700-1200 in summer. *Banks:* 0830-1200 Sunday to Wednesday. Business hours: 0800-1300 and 1600-1900 Sunday to Wednesday 0800-1300 on Thursday. *Oil companies:* 0700-1500 Sunday to Thursday. *British Embassy in Abu Dhabi and Dubai:* 0730-1430 Saturday to Thursday. *British Consulate:* 0800-1300 Sunday to Thursday. Working hours are modified during the holy month of Ramadan.

U
A
E

Currency

UAE Dirham (AED) divided into 100 fils. The AED is tied to the US$ at US$1 = AED 3.672. At the time of going to print, the exchange rate was AED 5.97 = £1 sterling. Credit cards are widely accepted and most major banks are linked to at least one international ATM network.

Income Tax

There is no personal taxation in UAE.

Electricity Supply

240 volts in Abu Dhabi and 220 volts in Dubai and the Northern Emirates. Plugs are three-pin flat or round.

Transportation

Most hotels have an airport pick up service. Taxis are numerous and inexpensive. Taxis have meters in both Abu Dhabi and Dubai. In Abu Dhabi, the visitor requires an International Driving Licence to hire a car. In Dubai, a UK Driving Licence is acceptable although most hire companies prefer an International Licence. In the other Emirates a UAE Driving Licence is necessary for visitors and resident expatriates. This can be obtained from the Traffic Department. Under UAE law a driver must stay at the scene of an accident and not move the vehicle until the police arrive. Penalties for driving while under the influence of alcohol are particularly severe. Chauffeur-driven limousines are reasonably priced and often considered more convenient for visitors on business. In the border areas of the Northern Emirates or Buraimi, drivers should ensure they have vehicle insurance cover for Oman if there is any likelihood that they will cross the Omani border, however briefly. National airlines are Etihad Airways which operates out of Abu Dhabi, Emirates Airlines owned by and operated out of Dubai and Gulf Air owned jointly by Abu Dhabi, Bahrain and Oman.

Tipping

Taxis are not tipped. Hotels and restaurants normally add a service charge although this goes to the restaurant, not to the waiter. The rate for airport porters is up to Dhs 5 depending on the number of pieces of baggage.

Embassies

Embassy of the United Arab Emirates in UK
30 Princes Gate, London SW7 1PT
Tel: 020 7581 1281/4113; Fax: 020 7481 9616*Embassy of the United Arab Emirates in US*
Suite 600 [check] New Hampshire Avenue NW,
Washington DC 20007 Tel: (202) 338 6500.
British Embassies in the United Arab Emirates
Abu Dhabi (Resident Ambassador), Khalid bin Waleed St (Street 22) PO Box 248, Abu Dhabi Tel: 00 971 2 6101100
Website: http://ukinuae.fco.gov.uk
Dubai (Resident Consul-General) British Embassy, Al-Seef Road, PO Box 65. Dubai.
Tel: 00 971 4 309 4444 Fax 00 971 4 309 4301
US Embassy in Abu Dhabi
Sudan Street, Abu Dhabi and
US Consulate General in Dubai
Website: http://uae.usembassy.gov

Tourist Sites and Activities

The many sites of interest in Abu Dhabi include the Al-Husn Palace (The Old Fort), the oldest building in the city, excellent restaurants in the large hotels, on the breakwater, in the port or aboard a dhow, some of which have live entertainment. There is also fishing, ice skating, scuba diving, camel racing and a polo club. There are a number of topical events of interest such as the annual boat race and if time permits, a visit to Al-Ain and Buraimi is well worthwhile. In Dubai, which is one of the world's most popular tourist destinations, there are luxurious hotels and beach resorts, international standard golf clubs, horse racing, water sports, excellent restaurants and live evening entertainment. Among the tourist sites are the excellent Dubai museum, Shaikh Saeed's House (the great-grandfather of the present ruler), the *souq*, the traditional buildings with their wind towers, the creek crossing on an *abra* boat (meaning

213

'across'in Arabic) or hiring an *abra* for a short tour of the waterfront. There are also numerous sites of interest in the Northern Emirates, the mountains and beaches of which are popular picnic spots.

General Comments

The UAE is among the most relaxed of the Peninsula states for a Westerner to visit. Thoroughly modern and catering for many tastes it nevertheless retains its very distinctive Arab culture, and the underlying society is conservative, well-ordered and always in accordance with the tenets of Islam. Western visitors are, of course, expected to fully respect the Islamic culture in their general behaviour and in such matters as dress in public places.

Further Information
FCO Country Profile and particularly Travel Advice: www.fco.gov.uk
UK Trade & Investment Country Profile: www.uktradeinvest.gov.uk
The United Arab Emirates, The Business Traveller's Handbook, published by Gorilla Guides ISBN: 1 903185 025
Lonely Planet *Oman, UAE and Arabian Peninsular Travel Guide* 2007 ISBN: 9781741045468

The Republic of Yemen

Geography

The Republic of Yemen occupies the southwestern corner of the Arabian Peninsula covering an area of about 530,000 sq kms, bordering the Red Sea in the west, Saudi Arabia in the north, Oman in the east and the Gulf of Aden and the Arabian Sea in the south. There are four distinct geographical regions: along the Red Sea coast lies the Tihama, a semi-desert strip up to 50 kms wide. Inland of this is a mountainous region which rises to over 3000m above sea level in places before giving way to fertile uplands at around 2000 meters. The eastern part of the country is mainly desert, including part of the Rub'Al-Khali (The Empty Quarter) and the south a mixture of mountains and desert. Yemen's capital city Sana'a (and its international airport) is situated inland in the fertile uplands at around 2000m above sea level. It has over a million inhabitants. Aden, the second city and main port, also with an international airport and the location of the Aden Free Zone, lies on the southern coast. It has a population of around 450,000. Aden is 363 kilometers from Sana'a. Other major towns include Al-Hudaidah, the country's main Red Sea port and Tai'z, previously the capital of the Yemen Arab Republic (North Yemen), situated 256 kms south of Sana'a. Tai'z is Yemen's most industialised city with about 500,000 inhabitants. In the eastern governorates of the Hadhramaut are the ancient city of Shabwa and the Arabian Sea port of Al-Mukalla

Climate

The Tihama and the southern coastal strip is generally hot, humid and dusty with daytime temperatures averaging 36°C in winter and 40°C and above in summer. Rainfall is low. The highlands have a mild climate with

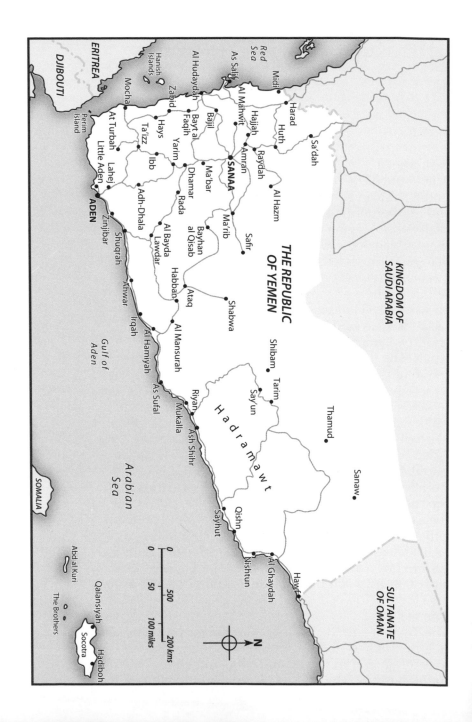

daytime temperatures between 25 and 30°C. The winters can be cold, particularly at night when temperatures fall to 0°C. Most rain falls in the western mountains, mainly in July and August.

History

Home to a number of civilisations and kingdoms since the 11th century BC, the region prospered until the 4th Century AD because of the development of overland trade routes to the north and also because of its agriculture, as the main source of frankincense and myrrh. This was the land described by the Romans as Arabia Felix and the country of the Queen of Sheba. In the 7th century the area converted to Islam. There followed a series of Yemeni rulers and dynasties, prominent among them the Zaydi and the Kathirid, until the arrival of the Portuguese in the region. They were supplanted by the Ottoman Turks in the 16th Century who were in turn ousted by the Zaydi Imams (religious leaders of the Zaydi dynasty). From 1839 Britain, anxious to protect its strategic route to India, eventually colonised Aden and entered into protectorate relations with the adjacent Shaikhdoms (the area previously known as South Yemen). The Ottomans returned to occupy the Yemeni highlands (North Yemen) until at the end of World War I they were finally ousted by the Zaydi Imans. In 1962 an army coup overthrew the Imamate in a revolution and established the Yemen Arab Republic (YAR). There followed a bitter eight-year civil war between Republican and Royalist Forces in which Egypt and Russia supported the Republicans. However, in 1967 the Egyptians withdrew and in 1970 the conflict was resolved. Meanwhile in the south, a nationalist (Marxist) movement in Aden and the surrounding Protectorates fomented the outbreak of a guerrilla war which led to the withdrawal of the British in 1967 and the formation in 1970 of the People's Democratic Republic of Yemen (PDRY). On 22 May 1990 the two Yemens, north and south, became a single nation state for the first time in their history and the Republic of Yemen was formed.

Although there has been a brief period of civil conflict, internal unrest, terrorist incidents and lawlessness since that time, the Government continues to promote reconciliation between north and south, striving for political stability and improved internal security. (see *General Comments,* including advice on personal security, below).

Government
The Republic of Yemen is a democracy. The elected Head of State is President Ali Abdullah Saleh who has held that position since unification in 1999. The Prime Minister is Dr Abdul Qadir Bajammal. The ruling political party is the General Peoples Congress (GPC). Other parties are Islah and the Yemeni Socialist Party (YSP). The Government is pursuing a policy of decentralisation. The tribal tradition however, also remains strong, particularly in rural areas.

Economy
The Republic of Yemen is in the initial stage of a major economic reconstruction and development programme supported by the World Bank, the IMF and other donors. Oil was discovered in the early 1980s and although it makes the major contribution to Government revenue, is limited in production and reserves, and vulnerable to fluctuating prices. There is scope for further expansion of the oil and particularly the gas industries, but there is also a need to develop existing industries and diversify the economy. Opportunities for development are possible in the fields of agriculture, fishing, mining, construction, local crafts and the shipping and logistics industries centred on Aden's harbour and free port. Aden is the Yemen's principal economic and commercial centre and most foreign companies operating in the country are based there. Although the internal security situation has hampered progress and deterred investors, the Government has achieved significant reforms in recent years which if continued, and combined with an improvement in the security situation, will eventually lead to the economy realising its full potential.

Y
E
M
E
N

Conduct of Business
Although not legally required in all cases, it is generally advisable for Western businessmen wishing to access the market to appoint a reliable local agent or distributor. The Yemen Government encourages franchising, joint ventures and manufacturing under licence.

Population
The population is estimated at 20 million with an annual growth rate of 3.7%. It is a strongly tribal society. The tribes and a number of ethnic groups influence the political groupings and Government policy.

Religion
The state religion is Islam. Almost all Yemenis are Muslims, fairly evenly divided between followers of the Zaydis, a Shia Grouping, predominant in the former YAR and the Shafi, a Sunni grouping predominant in the former PDRY.

Official Language
Arabic. English is the second language and is widely spoken in business circles.

National Flag
Divided into three horizontal stripes – red (top), white and black.

Visas
British citizens visiting Yemen require a visa and although it is possible for British and EU citizens travelling as part of a tour group or with a letter of invitation to obtain a visa at the airport upon arrival, the FCO advise obtaining it before departure. Application should be made well in advance, to a Yemen Embassy abroad. Visit visas are normally valid for a month and can be extended in-country for another month, although it is then necessary to apply for a (free) exit permit. Travellers with evidence in their passports of visits to Israel are liable to be refused entry.

Alcohol
The importation of alcohol is prohibited, as are goods from Israel.

Local Time GMT + 3 hours, EST + 8 hours

Dialling Code
00 967. Area codes are: Sana'a 1, Aden 2, Hodeidah 3, Tai'z 4, Mukalla 5.

Public Holidays
All Muslim Festivals (*see* Chapter 1), May Day – 1 May, National Day – 22 May, September Revolution – 26 September, October Revolution – 14 October and Independence Day – 30 November.

Working Hours
Government offices: 0800-1500 Saturday to Wednesday and 0800-1130 on Thursday. Banks: 0830-1200 Saturday to Wednesday and 0800-1130 Thursday.
Business: 0800-1200 Saturday to Wednesday and 0800-1130 Thursday.
Banks: 0830-1200 Saturday to Thursday.
Shops: 0800-1300 and 1600-2100 Sunday to Thursday.
British Embassy – Sana'a and the British Consulate: 0730-1430 Saturday to Wednesday. Working hours are modified during the Holy month of Ramadan.

Currency
The Yemeni Riyal (YER) is divided into 100 fils. At the time of going to print, the exchange rate was YER 324 = £1 sterling and YER 200 = US$1. Credit cards are only accepted in the largest hotels. Local banks will not advance cash against credit cards. ATMs are scarce. It is advisable to carry US$ as a readily convertible currency.

Health
It is important to seek advice on health matters prior to travel. Vaccination against yellow fever is required if arriving within six days of leaving or transiting

an infected area, and malarial prophylactics are recommended for those visiting the Tihama region on the Red Sea and the coastal strip on the Gulf of Aden. Those with a heart condition or high blood pressure who intend visiting Sana'a, Taiz or other areas at high altitude should consult their doctor before travelling and are advised to take moisturising cream, lip salve and sun cream. It is advisable to drink bottled water. Medical facilities outside the main towns are poor. In the event of an emergency, British nationals can contact the Consular Section of the British Embassy in Sana'a or the Consulate-General in Aden for advice about suitable doctors and dentists in Sana'a, Aden and Taiz.

Security
It is important to seek the latest travel advice, including the security situation, prior to travel, particularly the FCO's website advice. One may also contact the Birtish Embassy in Sana'a and UK Trade & Investment (see details below). On arrival in Yemen, British nationals should register with the British Embassy.

Personal Taxation
There is an upper income tax level for non-residents of 35%.

Electricity Supply
220/230 volts AC, 50 Hz, with 2-pin plugs.

Transportation
Taxis have yellow licence plates. They do not have meters and the fare should be negotiated before each journey. The fare from Sana'a and Aden airports to each of the city centres costs up to US$10. The national airline, Yemenia, flies twice weekly direct to Sana'a from London's Gatwick Airport.

Tipping
Although service is included in hotel and restaurant bills it is customary to tip between 10% to 15%. This is also the case with taxis.

Embassies

Embassy of the Republic of Yemen in UK
57 Cromwell Road, London SW7 2ED
Tel: 020 7584 6607, Fax: 020 7589 3350
Embassy of The Republic of Yemen in US
Suite 705, 2600 Virginia Avenue NW, Washington DC 20037
Tel: (202) 965 4760 Fax: (202) 837 2017
Consulate of The Republic of Yemen in US
United Nations Plaza, New York NY 10017
Tel: (212) 355 1730 Fax: (212) 750 9613
British Embassy in The Republic of Yemen
938 Thaher Himiyar Street,
East Ring Road opposite Movenpick Hotel
PO Box 1287 Sana'a,Tel: (+ 967) 1 308100
Fax: (+967) 1 302 454
Website: http://ukinyemen.fco.gov.uk
US Embassy in The Republic of Yemen
Sa'wan Street Sana'a. Tel: 00 967 1 303155.
Website: http://yemen.usembassy.gov

Tourist Sites

Tourism is in its infancy and precluded at the time of going to print by the internal security situation. However, when it is again feasible. visitors are likely to be fascinated by the Yemen's ancient culture and enthralled by its architecture, from the low painted houses of the Tihama to the famous tower houses built of stone, mud or mud brick of the highlands, each floor with its own function as home for the animals, *majlis*, bedrooms, etc. Sites of interest in Sana'a include the Old City, the National Museum and the mosques. Also the Souq Al-Milh, meaning Salt Souq but actually a collection of around forty different souqs. Outside Sana'a the sites include the fertile Wadi Dahr, Shibam (not to be confused with Shibam in the Hadhramaut), and Kawkaban. Further afield, Ta'iz and in the Hadhramaut, the ancient cities of Shabwa, Shibam and Al-Mukalla. Further information can be obtained from the office of the General Tourist Corporation in Sana'a at the western end of Maidan At-Tahir.

General Comments
Prior to travel, it is important to seek the latest travel advice, particularly on the security situation, given on the FCO website. On arrival in Yemen, British nationals should register with the British Embassy.

Further Information
FCO Country Profile and particularly Travel Advice: www.fco.gov.uk
UK Trade & Investment Country Profile: www.uktradeinvest.gov.uk
Lonely Planet *Oman, UAE & Arabian Peninsula Travel Guide* September 2007 ISBN: 9781741045468

Y
E
M
E
N

FCO travel advice and consular assistance abroad

General

The FCO website www.fco.gov.uk gives the latest advice on travel to individual countries or telephone the Travel Advice Unit on 0870 606 0290. In addition, the business traveller can obtain guidance from the FCO's Security Information Service for Businesses Overseas (SISBO), (details on the FCO website) or contact the Business Team in the Global Business Group in FCO Email: peter.obrien@fco.gov.uk or Tel: 020 7008 3675. SISBO co-ordinators are also located in all British embassies in the Peninsula.

FCO travel advice includes the purchase of tickets, money, Insurance, health, avoiding trouble spots, security, obeying the law, drugs, alcohol, driving and what to do if you are arrested, have something stolen or if someone should die. It advises noting the address and telephone number of the British Embassy and Consulate.

British Consulates Abroad

The FCO website also includes information on Consular services abroad (Tab 'If it all goes wrong'). It advises that Consulates do everything they properly can to help British people in difficulty abroad. It lists what Consulates currently can and cannot do for you:

Consulates can:
- Issue emergency passports, and in some places full passports;
- Contact relatives and friends and ask them to help you with money or tickets;
- Tell you how to transfer money;
- In an emergency, cash you a sterling cheque worth up to £100 in local currency, if supported by a valid banker's card;

- Help you get in touch with local lawyers, interpreters and doctors;
- Arrange for next of kin to be told of an accident or a death and advise on procedures;
- Visit you if you have been arrested or put in prison, and arrange for messages to be sent to relatives and friends;
- Put you in touch with organisations who help trace missing persons;
- Speak to the local authorities on your behalf;
- Only as a last resort, in exceptional circumstances, and as long as you meet certain strict rules, give you a loan to get you back to the UK, but only if there is no-one else who can help you.

UK law obliges Consulates to charge for some services and they display the current fees and the standards of service they aim to maintain.

Consulates cannot:

- Get you out of prison;
- Give legal advice or start court proceedings for you;
- Get you better treatment in hospital or prison than is given to local nationals;
- Investigate a crime;
- Pay your hotel, legal, medical or any other bills;
- Pay your travel costs, except in special circumstances;
- Do work normally done by travel agents, airlines, banks or motoring organisations;
- Get you somewhere to live, a job or work permit;
- Demand you be treated as British if you are a dual national in the country of your second nationality. (More information on dual nationality is given on the website.)

Commercial support for US companies

General Information
For general information about US Government export promotion programmes, contact the Trade Information Center which provides information on Federal programmes and activities that support US exports, information on overseas markets and industry trends, as well as a computerised calendar of US Government sponsored domestic and overseas trade events. The Center's nationwide toll-free number is: 1-800-USA-TRADE(1-800-872-8723) or visit www.export.gov (information on US Government activity in Iraq is given on www.export.gov/iraq).

Specific Information and Support
The start point for any US company considering doing business in the countries of the Peninsula would be their local US Export Assistance Center of the International Trade Administration, US and Foreign Commercial Service of the US Department of Commerce.

Directory of Export Assistance Centers
The list of US Department of Commerce, Export Assistance Centers is given on website www.export.gov/comm_svc/eac.html.

US and Foreign Commercial Service Abroad
The US and Foreign Commerical Service is represented in the US Embassies of all important market locations. They pull together local information and undertake basic commercial research in local markets in support of US-Arab trade. Much of this research information is provided to US companies free of charge, unless they have incurred significant expense in the process, in which

case a nominal charge is made. In addition, the Foreign Commercial Service offer a direct market service, support the various Economic Development Groups and Trade Promotion Missions and provide a Gold Key Service to individual US small- to medium-sized companies under which, on payment of a fee, the US and Foreign Commercial Service will advise on specific markets, support a company visit and make appointments in-country.

Contact details for US Embassies in the Peninsula states are given in the relevant Country Annexes.

US SUPPORT

GLOSSARY

abaya	Traditional long black cloak worn by Muslim women in the Peninsula.
Abdul	'Servant of', e.g. Abdul-Rahmaan - 'Servant of the Merciful' (*see* page 82).
Abu	'Father of' (*see* page 84).
Ad-Din	'Of the faith' (*see* page 84).
Akhee	'My brother'. Traditional way of referring to a friend.
Al or *El*	Definite article.
Allah	The Muslim word for God, which means 'the God'.
Amir	Ruler (Kuwait and Qatar).
aqaal	Head rope, originally double-looped used for hobbling camels.
baksheesh	A tip.
Bedu	Sing. *Bedouin*, 'a nomadic desert dweller'.
bin	'Son of', used with the father's and grand-father's name, e.g. Mohammed bin Ahmed bin Abdullah. Also written *ibn*.
bint	'Girl' or 'daughter'. Used in a name in the same way as *bin* or *ibn*.
birka	Veil covering the whole of a Muslim woman's face, except for the eyes. Also called *hijab*.

bisht	Kuwaiti and Saudi term for the traditional outer robe or cloak. Also called a *mishlah* and often trimmed with gold when worn by distinguished citizens, shaikhs, etc.
burga	Mask covering lower part of face of a veiled Muslim woman.
Caliph	Literally, 'successor'. Title adoped by leaders of the Muslim community after the death of the Prophet Muhammad.
dinar	Unit of currency in Iraq, Kuwait and Bahrain.
dirham	Unit of currency in the UAE.
dishasha	Kuwaiti term for the full length, long cotton robe worn throughout the Peninsula. Also called a *thobe* in Saudi Arabia and the Gulf.
Eid Al-Adha	The festival celebrating the end of the Pilgrimage at which all pilgrims offer a sacrifice to God.
Eid Al-Fitr	The festival celebrating the end of the month-long fast of Ramadan.
fatwa	Religious edict issued by the *Ulema* (religious scholars).
ghūtra	One term used for the headcloth worn in Saudi Arabia and the Gulf. Also called a *she**maag***.
Ha**dith**	Authenticated teachings, sayings and acts of the Prophet Muhammad and his Companions.
Hajj	The Pilgrimage to Makkah which, in accordance with the Five Pillars of Islam, must be made by every Muslim if he can afford it. The *Hajj* is made in the pilgrimage month which ends *Eid Al-Adha*.

Hajji	(fem. *Hajja*) Pilgrim. Title given to someone who has completed the pilgrimage to Makkah.
halaal	'Permitted'. Used to describe food which is allowed to Muslims, including animals slaughtered in the prescribed Islamic manner.
hijab	Veil covering the whole face of Muslim women, except the eyes – also called a *birka*.
Hijra	The 'migration 'in AD 622 when Muhammad fled to Medina. The official start of the Muslim era and calendar, described as Anno Hijra (AH).
ibn	'Son of', *see bin.*
Imaam	'He who goes before'. One who leads Muslims in prayer.
In-sha'Allah	'If God wills', often proclaimed by a Muslim to demonstrate his belief that every occurrence on earth is ordained by God.
Iqaama	Residence permit.
Jihad	Holy War. Used to cover any large-scale action, including war and economic sanctions, in which a whole Muslim community endeavours to achieve a religiously sanctified objective.
Ka'aba	The large cube-shaped monument in the Grand Mosque in Makkah, which is the focal point to which all Muslims pray. It is revered as the House of God built by Abraham. The Ka'aba is about 50 feet high and draped in rich black and gold hangings, which are renewed each year.
Koran	*see Quran (Holy).*

G
L
O
S
S
A
R
Y

kūfeeya   Small, white skullcap worn under the *gūtra/shemaag*.

majlis   Reception or meeting in an Arab house or palace. From the verb *jalas*, 'he sits down'.

Majlis As-Shura Consultative Council.

masjid   Mosque.

mihraab   Niche in mosque wall indicating the direction of Makkah.

minaara   Minaret.

minbar   Pulpit in mosque from which the oratory is given at Friday prayers.

mishlah   *See bisht.*

muezzin   Caller to prayer.

nargeela   Hubble-bubble. Smokers' pipe, burning various flavours of tobacco. The smoke is drawn through water along a long pipe.

Nasrani   Christian. Lit. 'a follower' of the man from Nazareth.

Qadi   Judge

qūbba'a   Small, round, woven hat in a variety of decorative colours, worn in Oman.

Quran (Holy)   Also spelt Koran. The Muslim holy book containing God's revelation to the Prophet Muhammad, set out in 114 *Suras* (*qv*). (*See* Chapter 1.)

Ramadan	The holy month of fasting *(Sawm)*, one of the Five Pillars of Islam. Commemorates the revelation of the Holy Quran by Allah to the Prophet Muhammad. Between dawn and dusk Muslims abstain from food, drink and all pleasurable pursuits.
riyal	Unit of currency in Saudi Arabia, Oman, Qatar and Yemen.
Rub' Al-Khali	The Empty Quarter. Derives from the term 'the barren lands', used by the Bedu to describe the immense desert in the south of Saudi Arabia.
rūkhsa	Leave or holiday.
Salah	Prayer. One of the Five Pillars of Islam.
Sawm	Fasting. One of the Five Pillars of Islam.
Shahaada	The Declaration of Faith. Lit. 'bearing witness'. One of the Five Pillars of Islam.
Shaikh	Hereditary title used by members of the ruling families of the Arab Gulf states. Also a title given to leaders of tribes, senior members of leading families, religious leaders and judges. Lit. 'old and revered person'. (Pronounced 'shake' not 'chic'.)
Shari'a	Islamic law.
shemaag	See *gūtra*.
Shia	Classification within Islam.
sooq	Market.
Sultan	Ruler (Oman).

GLOSSARY

Sunna	Lit. 'customary procedure'.
Sunni	Classification within Islam. The Sunni, or 'orthodox', follow the succession of the elected caliphate. The great majority of Arabs in the Arabian Peninsula are Sunni.
Sura	Chapter in the Holy Quran.
tafuddal	Used when offering someone something. Lit. 'be pleased to'.
thobe	*See dishdasha.*
Ulema	A grouping of Islamic scholars and/or dignitaries who hold an important position in Islam in most Islamic countries.
Umm	Mother. Also traditionally used to describe a woman as the mother of her eldest son, e.g. 'Umm Mohammed'.
wadi	Dry, stony river bed (except in the rainy season).
wosta	Influence.
wūdooh	Minor ablution.
Zakat	Almsgiving to the poor. A religious duty on all Muslims. One of the Five Pillars of Islam.

G
L
O
S
S
A
R
Y

Basic vocabulary

about	*howl*	back	*dhahr*
above	*foqe*	bad	*battaal*
accident	*haadith*	bag (paper)	*kees (aykaas)*
	(hawaadith)	bag (suitcase)	*shanta*
across	*aber*	Bahrain	*Al-Bahrayn*
adviser	*mūstashaar*	baker	*khabbaaz*
	(mūtashaareen)	bananas	*mooz*
after	*ba'ad*	bank	*baank*
afternoon/this	*ba'ad adh-dhūhr*	bar	*baar*
afternoon		barber	*hallaaq*
again	*murra* or	bazaar	*sooq*
	thaaneeya	bathroom	*hammaam*
against	*did*	beautiful	*jameel*
he agrees (on)	*yūwaafaq ala*	because	*leeyan*
he agreed (on)	*waafaq ala*	bed	*firaash*
air conditioner	*mūkayyif*	beer	*beera*
aircraft	*teiyaara*	before	*qobl*
air force	*sillah al-jow*	behind	*wora*
airport	*mataar*	belly dancer	*raaqisa sharqeeya*
all	*kūll*	beneath	*taht*
also	*eidan*	beside	*jamb*
always	*deiman*	better	*ahsan*
ambassador	*safeer (sūfara'a)*	between	*bayn*
America	*Amreeka*	big	*kabeer*
and	*wa*	bill (restaurant)	*hisaab*
angy	*za'laan*	bird	*tayr (tūyoor)*
animal	*heiyawaan*	black	*aswad*
	(heiyawaanaat)	blue	*azraq*
answer	*jowaab*	boat/ship	*markab*
antiques	*anteeqaat*		*(maraakib)*
apples	*tūffah*	boiled	*maslooq*
apricots	*mishmish*	book	*kitaab (kūtub)*
April	*Neesaan*	bookshop	*maktaba*
Arab	*Arabee (Arab)*	bowling	*booling*
Arab Gulf	*Al-Khaleej*	box	*sūndook*
	Al-Arabee		*(sanaadeek)*
army	*jeysh (jūyoosh)*	boy	*wulud (awlaad)*
assistant	*mūaawin*	brass	*nūhaas*
	(mūaawineen)	bread	*khūbz*
at	*eind*	bread (local)	*khūbz baladi*
attack	*hūjoom*	breakfast	*fūtoor*
August	*Aab*	bring me	*jeeblee*

235

VOCABULARY

Britain	*Bareetaaneeya*
British	*Bareetaanee*
broken	*maksoor*
brother	*akh (ikhwa)*
brown	*asmar*
brush	*fūrsha (fūrash)*
bus	*bus (busaat)*
bus stop	*mahattat al-bus*
businessman	*rajūl a'maal*
but	*laakin or walaakin*
butter	*zibda*
he buys	*yashtaree*
he bought	*ishtaraa*
by	*bi*
by car	*bi seiyaara*
cake	*kaa'k*
Cairo	*Al-Qaahira*
camel	*jamal (jimaal)*
camera	*aalat at-tasweer*
capital city	*aasima*
car	*seiyaara (seiyaaraat)*
card	*bitaaqa*
carpet	*sajjaada*
he carried	*hamal*
he carries	*yahmil*
case (legal)	*da'wa*
case (luggage)	*shanta*
castle/palace	*qal'a*
centre	*markaz (maraakiz)*
certainly	*ma'loom*
certificate	*shahaada*
chair	*kūrsee (karaasee)*
cheap	*rakhees*
cheaper	*arkhas*
cheese	*jubna*
chemist shop	*seidalleeya*
cheques	see *travellers' cheques*
chief	*ra'ees (ru'asaa)*
chicken	*dūjaaja*
Christian	*Maseehee (maseeheeyeen)*
church	*kaneesa*
cigarette	*sigaara*
circle	*daa'ira*
city	*madeena (mūdūn)*
clean	*nodheef*

he cleaned	*nodhdhaf*
he cleans	*yūnnadhif*
clever	*shaatir*
clock/hour	*saa'a (saa'aat)*
closed	*m'sukkar*
close (to)	*qoreeb (min)*
clothing	*libaas*
club	*naadee*
coast	*saahil*
coffee	*qahwa*
coffee-house	*maqha*
cold	*baarid*
college	*kūleeya*
colour	*lone (alwaan)*
commerce/trade	*tijaara*
complaint	*shakwa*
concerning	*bikhūsoos*
congratulations	*mabrook*
Consulate	*Consūleeya*
contract	*aqd (ūqood)*
cook	*tabbaakh*
correct	*saheeh*
cost	*qeema*
country	*bilaad (būldaan)*
crime	*jareema (jaraa'im)*
cross (n)	*saleeb*
crowd	*jūmhoor (jamaahir)*
cup	*finjaan (fanaajeen)*
custom	*aada (aadaat)*
customs (at airport)	*jūmrūk or jamaarik*
Damascus	*Dimashq*
dancing	*raqs*
danger	*khatar*
date	*taareekh*
date (edible)	*tamar (tūmoor)*
dawn	*fajar*
day (in a day)	*yome (ayaam)*
day before yesterday	*awal ams*
day after tomorrow	*ba'ad būkra*
daytime	*nahaar*
December	*Kaanoon Al-Awwal*
defence	*difaa'*
delicious	*lodheedh*

dentist	*tobeeb al-asnaan*	envelope	*dharf (dhŭroof)*
department	*daa'ira (dawaa'ir)*	equipment (piece of)	*jihaaz (ajhiza)*
desert	*baadia*		
deputy	*wokeel (wŭkalaa)*	equipment (military)	*ŭdd (ŭdad)*
dictionary	*qaamoos*		
the difference between	*al-farq bayn*	especially	*khŭsoosan*
		essential	*jawharee*
difficult	*sa'ab*	evening	*masaa*
direction	*jiha or ittijaah*	evening entertainment	*sahra*
director	*mŭdeer (mŭdara)*		
dirty	*wasakh*	every	*kŭll*
distance	*musaafa*	exactly	*tamaaman bidopt*
district	*mintaqa (manaatiq)*	for example	*mathalan*
division, part	*qism (aqsaam)*	except	*illa*
he did	*amil or sawwa*	excellent	*mŭmtaaz*
he is doing	*ya'mal*	exhibition	*ma'rid (ma'aarid)*
doctor	*tobeeb*	it existed	*wajad*
dog	*kalb (kilaab)*	it exists	*yoojad*
donkey	*himaar*	exit	*makhraj*
door	*baab (abwaab)*	expense	*masroof (massaareef)*
dress (general)	*libaas*		
dress (woman)	*fŭstaan (fasaateen)*	expensive	*ghaalee*
drink	*mashroob (mashroobaat)*	experiment	*tajriba (tajaarib)*
		expert (in)	*khabeer (bi)*
driver	*saa'iq (suwwaaq)*	explosion	*infijaar*
dry	*naashif*	exports	*saadiraat*
during	*khilaal*	external	*khaarijee*
dust	*tŭraab*	eye	*'ein ('ŭyoon)*
duty	*waajib (waajibaat)*		
		face	*wajh*
each of	*kŭl min*	family	*aa'ila*
early	*bakeer*	far...from	*ba'eed ...'an*
earth	*ardh*	fare (taxi)	*ŭjra*
east	*sharq*	fat (adj)	*sameen*
easy	*sahul*	Feast at end of Ramadan	*Eid Al-Fitr*
he ate	*akal*		
he eats	*yaakŭl*	February	*Shŭbaat*
egg	*bayda (bayd)*	festival	*eid*
Egypt	*Musr*	Festival of the Sacrifice	*Eid Al-Adha*
electricity	*kahraba*		
embassy	*sifaara*	few	*qoleel*
employee	*mŭwadhaf (mŭwadhdhafeen)*	figs	*teen*
		film	*film (aflaam)*
empty	*farrigh*	finally	*ukheeran*
end	*nihaaya*	finger	*ŭsbŭ (asaabi')*
engineer	*mŭhandis (mŭhandiseen)*	finish	*khalas*
		fire	*naar (fem)*
England	*Inglaterra*	fish	*samak*
English	*Ingleezee*	fishing	*sayd as-samak*

237

flag	*a'lam*	he goes out	*yakhrūj*
it flew	*taar*	he went out	*kharaj*
it flies	*yateer*	goat	*ma'z*
floor	*ardh*	God	*Allah*
floor (stony)	*taabūq*	gold	*dhahab*
floor show	*cabaaray*	golf	*goolf*
flower	*zahar (zūhoor)*	good	*teiyyib*
food	*akl*	government	*hūkooma*
foot	*qadam (aqdaam)*	green	*akhdhar*
for	*li*	group	*jamaa'a*
forbidden	*mamnoo'a*	guard (collective)	*haras*
foreign/foreigner	*ajnabee (ajaanib)*	guard	*haaris (hūrraas)*
he forgot/I forgot	*nasa/nasat*	(watchman)	
		guest	*dhayf (dhūyoof)*
he forgets	*yansa*	guide	*daleel*
France	*Faransa*	guidebook	*kitaab daleel*
free (at liberty)	*hūrr (ahraar)*	gulf	*khaleej*
free (of charge)	*majaanee*	gun	*madfa' (madaafi')*
French	*Fransaawee*		
Friday	*Yome al-Jūmaa*	hair	*sha'r*
friend	*sodeeq (asdiqaa)*	half	*nūss*
fried/roasted	*maqlee*	hand	*yad (aydin)*
from	*min*	handkerchief	*mandeel*
frontier	*hūdood*	happy	*fūrhaan*
fruit (pl)	*fawaakih*	harbour	*meena*
fuel	*wūqood*	hard	*sa'b*
full	*malyaan*	hat	*qūbba-a*
future	*mūstaqbil*	head	*raas*
		headcloth	*kūfeeyya*
gallon	*gaaloon*	headquarters	*qeeyaada*
garden	*būstaan* or *hadeeqa*	health	*sahha*
garment	*thawb (theeyaab)*	heart	*qolb*
gate	*baab (abwaab)*	heat	*haraara*
general (adj)	*aam*	heavy	*thaqeel*
generous	*kareem*	help	*awn* or *mūsaa'ada*
Germany	*Almaaneeya*	he helped	*saa'ad*
gift	*hadeeya (hadaayaa)*	he helps	*yūsaa'id*
		here	*hina*
girl	*bint (banaat)*	high	*aalee*
he gave	*a'taa*	hire	*eejaar*
he gives	*ya'atee*	he hired	*ista'jar*
glad	*farhaan*	he hires	*yasta'jir*
glass (drinking)	*kūbaaya*	holiday	*'ūtla*
glasses (spectacles)	*nadhaaraat*	honest	*ameen*
		horizontal	*ūfqee*
(go)he goes	*yarooh*	hors d'oeuvres	*mezza*
he went	*raah*	horse	*hisaan (husn)*
he goes in	*yadkhūl*	hot	*haar*
he went in	*dakhal*	hotel	*fūndūq (fanaadiq)*

238

hour	*saa'a (saa'aat)*	June	*Huzayraan*
house	*bayt (būyoot)*		
housewife	*sitt*	key	*miftaah*
how?	*kayf?*		*(mafaateeh)*
how many?	*kam?*	kilogram	*keelo*
how much?	*bi-kam?*	kilometre	*keelomitre*
hubble bubble	*nargeela*		*(keeloomitraat)*
hungry	*jo'aan*	kind (thoughtful)	*loteef*
hurry (in a)	*musta'jil*	king	*malik (mūlook)*
hunting	*sayd*	kingdom	*mamlaka*
husband	*zawj*	knife	*sikeen (sakaakeen)*
		he knew	*'araf*
ice	*thalj*	he knows	*ya'rif*
identity card	*hūweeya*	knowledge	*ilm*
if	*idha*		
ill	*mareedh*	last (adj)	*aakhir*
immediately	*haalan*	last week	*al-ūsboo'a al-*
important	*mūhim*		*maadhey*
imports	*waaridaat*	last year	*al-sana al-*
he imported	*istawrad*		*maadheeya*
he imports	*yastawrid*	late	*mūta'akhkhir*
in	*fee*	lately	*akheeran*
incident	*haadith*	law	*qaanoon*
	(hawaadith)		*(qawaaneen)*
India	*Al-Hind*	lazy	*kaslaan*
he informed	*khabir*	leader	*qaa'id (qūwaad)*
he informs	*yūkhbir*	Arab League	*Al-Jaami'a Al-*
information	*khabar*		*Arabeeya*
influence	*hibr*	left (opp. right)	*yesaar*
ink	*wosta*	leg	*rijl (arjul)*
inside	*daakhil*	lemon	*laymoon*
international	*dūwalee*	to let	*lil-eejaar*
invitation	*da'wa*	letter	*maktoob*
invitation card	*bitaaqat da'wa*	library	*maktaba*
is there?	*fee?*	life	*heiyaat*
island	*jazeera (jazaa'ir)*	lift (n)	*mas'ad*
			(masaa'id)
jacket	*jaaket or sūtra*	light (opp. dark)	*noor*
January	*Kanoon Ath-*	light (opp. heavy)	*khafeef*
	Thaani	like, as: such as	*mithl*
jewels	*jawaahir or*	he liked / loved	*habb*
	mūjawharaat	he likes / loves	*yahibb*
Jordan	*Al-Árdun*	little	*qoleel*
job	*wadheefa*	he looked around	*tafaaraj*
	(wadhaa'if)	he looks around	*yatafarraj*
journalist	*sahaafee*	love	*hūbb*
	(sahaafeeyeen)	lunch	*ghada*
July	*Tammooz*	machine	*makeena*
juice	*aseer*	mad	*majnoon*

239

magazine	*majalla*
man	*rajūl (rijaal)*
manager	*mūdeer*
many	*katheer*
map	*khaarita/khareeta*
March	*Aadhaar*
marine (or naval)	*bahree*
market	*sooq*
married	*mutazowwaj*
matches (pl. n)	*kabreet*
May	*Ayaar*
meat	*lahm*
meat spiced and grilled	*shawurma*
meeting	*ijtimaa' (ijtimaa'aat)*
melon	*botteekh*
merchant	*taajir (tujjaar)*
message	*risaala (rasaa'il)*
metre	*mitar (amtaar)*
middle	*wost*
Middle East	*Ash-Sharq Al-Owsat*
military (adj) (*lit.* defence)	*difaa'ee*
milk	*haleeb*
million	*milyoon*
minaret	*manaara*
minister	*wozeer (wuzaraa)*
ministry	*wizaara*
Ministry of	*Wizaarat...*
Agriculture	*Az-Ziraa'a*
Aviation	*At-Teiyaaraan*
Commerce	*At-Tijaara*
Communications	*Al-Mūwaasillaat*
Education	*At-Tarbeeya*
Defence	*Ad-Difaa*
Development	*Al-I'maar*
Finance	*Al-Maaleeya*
Foreign Affairs	*Al-Khaarijeeya*
Health	*As-Sahha*
Industry	*As-Sinaa'a*
Interior	*Ad-Daakhileeya*
Labour	*Al-Amal*
Marine	*Al-Bahreeya*
(Public) Works	*Al-Ashghaal (Al-Aamma)*
Transport	*An-Naqleeyaat*
minute	*daqeeqa (daqaa'iq)*
mistake	*ghalat (aghlaat)*
modern	*hadeeth*
moment	*lahdha (lahdhaat)*
Monday	*Yome al-Ithnayn*
money	*feloos*
month	*shahr (shūhoor)*
moon	*qamr*
morning	*sabaah*
Morocco	*Al-Maghrib*
mosque	*masjid*
most of	*aghlab min*
mountain	*jebal (jebaal)*
Mr	*seiyyid* or *meester*
much	*katheer*
music	*moozeeqa*
Muslim	*Mūslim (Muslimeen)*
name	*ism (asmaa)*
navy	*bahreeya*
near (to)	*qareeb (min)*
necessary	*dharooree*
neighbour	*jar (jeeraan)*
never	*abadan*
new	*jadeed*
news	*khabar (akhbaar)*
newspaper	*jareeda*
next week	*al-ūsboo'a al-jaiy*
next year	*as-sana al-jaiy*
night	*layl (layaali)*
no	*laa*
noise	*sawt*
noon	*dhuhr*
north	*shimaal*
notebook	*daftar (dafaatir)*
November	*Tishreen ath-Thaanee*
now	*alaan*
number	*raqm (arqaam)*
October	*Tishreen Al-Awwal*
office	*maktab (makaatib)*
oil (petroleum)	*naft*
oil (vegetable or lubricating)	*zayt*
old	*qodeem*
olives	*zaytoon*
on	*ala*
onions	*busal*

on the subject of	*bi-khūsoos*	porter	*hammaal*
only	*foqot/bass*	possible	*mūmkin*
open	*maftooh*	post	*bareed*
opportunity	*fūrsa*	post office	*maktab al-bareed*
or	*aw*	potatoes	*bataata*
oranges	*būrtūqaal*	pound (money)	*jūnayh*
other	*aakhar (fem.ūkhra)*	pound (weight)	*ratl*
outside	*kharij*	present (adj)	*haalee*
over (above)	*ala/foqe*	present/gift	*hadeeya*
			(hadaayaa)
pain	*waj'a*	Prime Minister	*Ra'ees al-Wūzara*
palace	*qala*	press (n)	*sahaafa*
Palestine	*filasteen*	principal (main)	*ra'eesee*
paper (piece of)	*woroqa (awraaq)*	problem	*mūshkila*
park	*būstaan*		*(mashaakil)*
Parliament	*barlamaan*	prohibited	*mamnoo'a*
part (of)	*juz (ajzaa) (min)*		
party	*hafla (haflaat)*	qualification	*salaaheeya*
political party	*hizb (ahzaab)*		*(salaaheeyaat)*
passenger	*raakib (rūkkaab)*	queen	*malika*
passport	*jawaaz*	question	*su'aal (as'ila)*
	(jawaazaat) Safar	quickly	*bisir'a*
past	*maadee*	quiet	*haadee*
the past	*al-maadee*	Quran, the Holy	*Al-Qūraan Al-*
peace	*silm* or *salaam*		*Kareem*
pen	*qolum hibr*		
pencil	*qolum rūsaas*	rain	*matar*
people (collect.)	*naas*	razor blades	*moos hallaaka*
the (or a)	*(ash-)sha'b*	ready	*haadhir*
people		reason	*sabab (asbaab)*
pepper	*filfil*	recent	*akheer*
perhaps/possibly	*yimkin*	red	*ahmar*
period	*mūdda*	Red Sea	*Al-Bahr Al-Ahmar*
permission/	*rūkhsa*	religion	*deen*
permit		rent	*eejaar*
person	*shakhs (ashkhaas)*	repair	*tasleeh*
petrol	*benzeen*	he repaired	*sallah*
photography	*soora (suwar)*	he will repair	*yūssalih*
pills	*hūboob*	reply	*jawaab (ajwiba)*
place	*mahal (mahallat)*	report (of	*taqreer (taqaareer)*
please	*mindfudlak*	committee)	
police	*shūrta/boolees*	request	*talab (talabaat)*
policeman	*shūrtee*	requested	*matloob*
police station	*mahattat ash-*	he requested	*talab*
	shūrta/boolees	he requests	*yatlūb*
poor	*faqeer (fūqaraa)*	reservation	*hajz*
pork	*lahm khanzeer*	he reserved	*hajaz*
port	*meena*	he reserves	*yahjaz*
	(mawaanee)	responsible (for)	*mas'ool (an)*

VOCABULARY

VOCABULARY

responsiblity	*mas'ooleeya*	at your service	*fee khidmatak*
rest (ease)	*raaha*	sheep (coll.)	*ghanam*
the rest of	*al-baaqee min*	Shaikh	*Shaykh (Shūyookh)*
restaurant	*mat'am (mataa'im)*	ship	*markab*
result (of)	*nateeja (min) (nataa'ij)*	shirt	*qomees*
		shoes	*ahdheeya* or *jazma (jizaam)*
he returned	*raja'*		
he returns	*yirja'*	shop	*dūkkaan (dakaakeen)*
rice	*ruz*		
rich	*ghanee*	shore	*shatt*
rifle	*būndūqeeya (banaadiq)*	short	*qaseer*
		shut	*mūsakkar*
right (opp. of left)	*yameen*	silver	*fidhdha*
		simple	*boseet*
river	*nahr*	since (time)	*mūndh*
room	*ghūrfa (ghūraf)*	slow (adj.)	*būtee'*
round (circular)	*mūdawwar*	small	*sagheer*
ruins	*aathar*	soldier	*jūndi (jūnood)*
ruler	*haakim*	some of	*ba'd min*
roast/fried	*maglee*	sometimes	*ihyaanan*
		soon (after a while)	*ba'd qaleel*
sad	*hazeen*		
safe (adj)	*saalim*	soup	*shoorba*
safe (n)	*khazna*	south	*jūnoob*
safety	*salaama*	he spoke	*takullum* or *haka*
salad	*salaata*	he speaks	*yatakallum* or *yihkee*
salt	*milh*		
sand	*raml*	specialist	*ikhsaa'ee*
Saturday	*Yome As-Sabt*	sport	*reeyaadha*
sauce/gravy	*salsa*	square (adj.)	*mūrubb'a*
Saudi Arabia	*Al-Mamlaka Al-Arabeeya As Sowdeeya*	stairs	*daraj*
		stamp (postage)	*taabi' (tawaabi'a)*
		star (lit. and fig.)	*najm (nūjoom)*
he said	*qaal*	station	*mahatta*
he says	*yaqool*	Sterling	*Isterleeney*
school	*madrassa (madaaris)*	step	*daraja*
		stomach	*botn*
sea	*bahr*	stone	*hajar (ahjaar)*
seat (chair)	*kūrsee*	street	*sharri' a*
secret (n.)	*sirr (asraar)*	strong	*qowee*
secret (adj.)	*sirree*	student	*taalib (tūllaab)*
secretary	*sikriteer (fem. sikriteera)*	sugar	*sūkkar*
		summer	*sayf*
he saw	*shaaf*	sun	*shams*
he sees	*yashoof*	Sunday	*Yome Al-Ahad*
September	*Aylool*	sweet	*hiloo*
servant	*khaadim (khūddaam)*	he swam	*sabah*
		he swims	*yasbah*
service	*khidma*	swimming pool	*masbaha*

table	*taawūla*	he travels	*yūsaafir*
tailor	*khayyaat*	travellers' cheques	*cheeqaat seeyaaha*
he talked	*takullum or haka*	tree	*shajara (ashjaar)*
he talks	*yatakullum or yakhee*	tribe	*qobeela (qabaa'il)*
		trousers	*bantaloon*
target	*hadaf (ahdaaf)*	true	*saheeh*
tax	*dareeba (daraaib)*	truth	*haqq*
tea	*shei*	Tuesday	*Yome Al-Thalaatha*
teacher	*mūdarris (mudarriseen) or mu'allim (mu'allimeen)*	type (mark)	*tiraaz*
		under	*taht*
		he understood	*fahim*
technical (adj.)	*fannee*	he understands	*yafhum*
technique	*fann (fūnoon)*	university	*jaami'a*
telegram	*telegraaf*	until	*hatta*
telephone	*telefoon*	up useful	*foqe*
temperature	*darajat al-haraara*	usual	*mūfeed*
tent	*khayma*	usually	*'aadi or 'aadatan*
there is / are	*fee*		
there was / were	*kaan fee*	valid	*jayyid*
that	*dhaalik*	valley (dry)	*waadee*
theatre	*masrah*	value	*qeema*
there	*hinaak*	valuable	*thameen*
thing	*shee (ashyaa)*	vegetables	*khūdra*
thirsty	*atshaan*	vertical	*amoodee*
this	*haadha*	very	*jiddan*
this morning	*haadha as-sabah*	village	*qoriya (qūraa)*
this afternoon	*ba'ad adh-dhu*hr*	he visited	*zaar*
thousand	*elf (aalaaf)*	he visits	*yazoor*
Thursday	*Yome Al-Khamees*		
time (period)	*woqt (awqaat)*	he waited	*intadhar*
time (occasion)	*murra (murraat)*	he waits	*yantadhir*
tired	*taa'baan*	he walked	*mashaa*
to	*ila*	he walks	*yimshee*
tobacco	*tombak*	wallet	*mahfaza*
today	*al-yome*	he wants	*yūreed*
toilet	*hammaam*	water	*moya/maa*
tomato	*tamaata*	weak	*da'eef*
tomorrow	*būkra*	weapon	*silaah (asliha)*
tomorrow night	*būkra fee-layl*	weather	*toqs*
toothbrush	*fūrsha lil-asnaan*	Wednesday	*Yome Al-Arba'a*
toothpaste	*ma'joon lil-asnaan*	week	*ūsboo'a*
tourism	*seeyaaha*	weight	*wazn*
tourist	*saa'ih (sūyaah)*	west	*gharb*
tourist office	*maktab as-seeyaaha*	what?	*aysh? or shoo?*
		when?	*aymta? or matta?*
towel	*manshafa*	where?	*wayn? or fayn?*
town	*balad*	which?	*ay?*
he travelled	*safar*	while	*baynamaa*

243

white	*abyad*	he wrote	***ka**tab*
who?	*meen?*	he writes	***yak**tūb*
whole	*kul*	writing paper	***wo**roq al-ki**taaba***
why?	*laysh?*	wrong (n.)	***gha**lat (a**ghlaat**)*
wind	*howa*	wrong (adj.)	*ghal**taan***
window	*shūb**baak***		
wine	*n**beedh***	year	*sana (si**neen**)*
winter	***shi**ta*	yellow	***as**far*
with	*ma*	Yemen	*Al-**Ye**man*
without	*bi**doon***	yes	***ei**wa or naam*
wireless	*la-**silkee***	yesterday	*ams*
woman	***hur**ma (ha**reem**)*	yoghurt	***la**ban*
word	***ka**lima (kali**maat**)*	young	*sa**gheer***
work	*shogl/amal*		
worker	*'**aa**mil/('aamal**leen***	zero	*sifr*
	or *'**ūm**maal**)*	zoological	*ha**dee**qat al-*
world	***aa**lam*	gardens	*heiyawaa**naat***

VOCABULARY

Index

I N D E X

INDEX

INDEX

I N D E X